FEMALE KILLERS: TRUE CRIME STORIES OF MURDEROUS WOMEN

**First edition. September 13, 2021.**

Copyright © 2021 Eliza Toska.

ISBN: 979-8201875909

Written by Eliza Toska.

# Table of Contents

# Female Killers: True Crime Stories of Murderous Women

By Eliza Toska

dimensionbooks.com

Although research, from a number of sources, has gone into this book, neither the author or publisher will be held responsible for any inaccuracies. To the best of the knowledge of the author and publisher, all information contained within this publication is factually correct, derived from researching these cases thoroughly.

This book is written in British English.

# Introduction

In the 1999 film *Girl, Interrupted*, Angelia Jolie's charismatic yet manipulative character, Lisa, said of being a sociopath, *"We are very rare and we are mostly men."*

This phrase is just as true when we're talking about women killers.

The fact that women make up just over a quarter of killers (*UK Parliament, 2021*) makes their crimes seemingly all the more shocking when they come to light. When their male counterparts rape, maim, shoot, stab, and wreak havoc in their killing endeavours, we are rightly shocked and disgusted. However, when a woman behaves the same, society seems to recoil all the more. It goes without saying all of the above acts are despicable and deserving of the harshest punishments, but we seem to have a much weaker stomach when it comes to digesting the abhorrent, vile behaviour of women.

This is perhaps because a murderous woman is a stark contrast to the "stereotypical woman" society views females as being; nurturing, caring, maternal, loving and empathetic. The truth is, women have been known to be just as evil, vengeful, cruel and violent as their male counterparts.

Regardless, it's still horrifying to hear stories like a nurse killing babies in her care, like Beverly Allitt, who senselessly snuffed out the lives of the very children she ought to protect. Or when learning about Cynthia Coffman or Myra Hindley, who both aided their partners in numerous rapes and murders. Then there's Stephanie Lazarus, a woman who committed a brutal murder before rapidly climbing the ranks in the LAPD, forcing you to confront the idea that even those whose job it is to protect us perhaps don't deserve 100% trust because of their position of supposed protection.

If you're intrigued by true crime like I am, then this compilation of cases will be sure to fascinate you.

# Karla Homolka

I recall hearing about this case many years ago when I first became fascinated with true crime, particularly serial killers. I was absorbed and horrified by the Karla Homolka story, and keen to know more about the case, I read and watched as much as I could find on the topic. I watched the film based on the killings, which was just as disturbing as I imagined it would be. Aware that the film would likely be free and easy with its artistic licence to perhaps lean away from the truth of the story, I also watched documentaries, read court transcripts and learned about Homolka's backstory, all in search of the answer to my question, '*Why?*'

Why would someone aid their partner in the rape and eventual murder of their sister? Why would someone help their deviant partner in videotaping the rape of young girls and even partake in the sexual assault itself? What makes someone such a willing accomplice in the cruel murders of innocent teenage girls?

While I don't have the definite answers to those questions (only opinions based on the facts - I'll let you make up your own mind as to why she did what she did), I do have a solid understanding of the horrific crimes that Karla Homolka so heartlessly carried out alongside her husband, Paul Bernardo.

Homolka was born May 4, 1970, in Ontario, Canada. She was, by all accounts, well-adjusted, attractive, intelligent, and popular. She had a loving, stable family life and plenty of friends, never showing any signs of the depravity she would unleash later on in her life. As she grew up, Homolka developed a love for animals, and when she finished high school, she went on to work at a veterinary clinic.

Homolka met Bernardo in 1987 when he was 23, and she was just 17. The teenager was in Toronto at a convention, and she and her friend got chatting to two men: Bernardo and his friend. Paul was handsome, with a thick mop of dirty blonde hair, piercing blue eyes and a golden tan, immediately piquing the interest of teenage Karla. Homolka and Bernardo hit it off straight away, leaving their respective friends with no choice but to talk to each other. That same day, the pair slept together for the first time. They soon discovered that they both had similar sadomasochistic inclinations, Paul taking on the role of master and Homolka becoming his willing slave.

The relationship was intense and moved quickly. Paul proposed to Karla on Christmas Eve and inserted himself into the Homolka family with ease. Karla's parents adored their soon-to-be son-in-law, and so did her younger sister, Tammy. Not only did Paul reciprocate Tammy's fondness, but he also took it further by flirting with the 15-year-old. The flirty banter wasn't just occasional, either - it was constant. Paul was attracted to the youngster, and Karla was all too aware of this. While jealous of her fiance's lust for another female - her kid sister no less - she was more than willing to help him act out his fantasies and participate in them.

Paul was frustrated at the fact that Karla wasn't a virgin when they met. That meant Paul felt it was Karla's responsibility to help facilitate his rape of Tammy, who was a virgin. There was a problem, though; Tammy couldn't know that her virginity was being stolen. She was to remain unaware she was being raped.

One can only imagine the conversations that were had when Paul pitched his sick rape plans to Karla. Instead of recoiling in disgust and heading to the police, Karla was on board with the sick idea. The pair plotted and came up with a fool-proof plan, even agreeing to videotape the attack.

With Karla working in a veterinary clinic, she had a fundamental knowledge of sedatives when using them on animals. The trick was working out how much to use to be able to knock Tammy out so she had no clue she was being raped. They needed to get the dose right so she would wake up with nothing but a mild hangover. In the end, Karla chose to use halothane, an anaesthetic for animals before they go through surgery. Tammy would be Paul's gift for Christmas.

However, there were some obstacles to overcome; the wicked pair didn't have the right equipment to get the halothane into the teenager's system, so Karla would have to hold a rag soaked in the anaesthetic over Tammy's face as the rape was carried out. She'd just have to make sure that she held that rag in such a way that her little sister could still breathe throughout the attack.

The date was set: December 23, 1990. The Homolka clan and Paul enjoyed food and drinks, with Paul getting out his camcorder to take videos of his in-laws and their daughters, Tammy, Lori and of course Karla. Paul's excitement was building; he was finally going to get what he'd lusted after for so long.

Paul spiked Tammy's alcoholic drinks with another sedative, Halcion. The effects were swift, and Tammy passed out on the couch after a couple of laced drinks. No doubt, the effects of alcohol helped speed up the effects of the drugs she was unwittingly fed, particularly since the young girl hadn't had much experience with booze. Eventually, Karla's mother and father called it a night and went to bed, which is when the pair pounced on their teenage target. Paul turned his camera on and held it above Tammy as he raped her, while Karla stood above them, holding the halothane rag over her little sister's face. Paul then insisted Karla had to join in. She obliged by making sexual advances to her heavily drugged sister.

After a short while, Tammy began throwing up. Ideally, Karla and Paul would have made sure the girl hadn't eaten before they'd carried out their sinister plan, but they took what they could get. There was no way to stop her eating at a family meal, after all. Karla used her veterinary knowledge to try and stop her sister from choking on her vomit - she held her upside down as she tried to clear her throat.

Her attempts were in vain. Tammy tragically - and senselessly - choked to death. Karla's amateur attempt at saving her sister's life had failed, so the callous couple worked quickly to dress Tammy and position her as naturally as they could. They hid the drugs used to sedate her, made sure the camera was out of sight and called an ambulance. The first that Karla's parents knew of the tragic death of their child was when they heard the sound of the ambulance pulling up outside. Everybody believed that Tammy died accidentally by choking on her vomit after too many eggnogs. Only two people knew the horrifying truth, but this wouldn't deter them from their deviant behaviour - if anything, it propelled it. Paul now needed a new girl to act out his depraved fantasies on.

Until then, he had Karla. Unlike other girls Paul had dated, Karla actually encouraged his sadistic side, particularly sexually. He would handcuff her, subdue her and ask her what she would think if he were a rapist. Her response was that it would be cool. Their bond strengthened, and Paul's lust for rape deepened. With Karla's approval, he started stalking and raping women at an alarming rate.

His modus operandi was often the same. His victim would get off a bus and he would stalk her, grabbing her from behind when the moment was right. He would drag the woman to the ground and force himself upon her in every way imaginable. He would flee the scene when he was done, leaving the victim alive but, of course, forever changed. Over the course of two years, his attacks on women reached double digits. He took a couple of month hiatus - possibly out of fear of being caught, or perhaps any victims during this period weren't identified. Still, he resumed his attacks on women in 1988.

Police had no clue who the 'Scarborough Rapist' was despite the abundance of physical evidence and victim descriptions of the attacker. Because of this, they managed to come up with a fairly accurate composite drawing of the rapist who had assaulted over a dozen women - and counting. The police distributed the composite sketch with the forces in the area, but it wasn't released to the public right away.

After every violent rape Paul carried out, he returned home to his doting wife and told her all about it. His vile stories of brutal sexual assaults were met with encouragement from Karla. One of Paul's victims recalled that during the attack, she saw a woman, apparently in cahoots with the rapist. Not only was this woman accompanying the rapist on his violent escapade, but she was also holding a video camera in her hands. When the woman told police about the rapist's accomplice, they brushed off her story as hysteria. In reality, the cruel pair were extremely partial to videoing their brutal assaults to watch back and revel in the victims' agonising torment.

Karla lived to make Paul happy; in fact, she was obsessed with him being happy, no matter what lengths she had to resort to in order to ensure his contentment. Her biggest fear in life was losing her husband-to-be, so whenever she felt him becoming distant or bored, she'd lure him back by doing something to excite him. Or rather, she'd find him *someone else* to get excited about.

Paul was still wounded that Tammy was no longer around to act out his sexual perversions and was vocal about this to Karla. He even blamed her for causing her little sister's death. Karla scrambled to replace Tammy - someone who was Paul's type; young, innocent and a virgin. She knew someone who fit the bill, a young girl only publicly named as Jane, who resembled Tammy in appearance. In Jane, Karla had found her wedding gift to Paul.

Jane saw Karla as something of a role model; beautiful, womanly, and sophisticated. She eagerly accepted Karla's invite to the couple's new house at 57 Bayview. Karla proceeded to take an impressionable young Jane out to dinner and spent hours talking with her (read: grooming her) and topping up the cocktails she was drinking. Eventually, Jane passed out from all the Halcion-laced booze and fell into a deep slumber.

Karla then called Paul to come and retrieve his surprise pre-wedding gift. To say he was pleased could be an understatement; he was especially thrilled when he noticed just how much Jane looked like Tammy. On top of that, Jane was a virgin to boot. For Paul, this was the perfect victim. Still, he showed some concern over Karla using halothane on the young girl - this was the drug that had killed Tammy. Karla eased Paul's worries and told him she was in control of the situation this time. It didn't take too much convincing from Karla to change Paul's mind. The pair quickly got to work undressing Jane.

With the young girl naked, Paul pulled out his camera. He filmed Karla as she raped the fifteen-year-old girl. Then it was Paul's turn. He took Jane's virginity and it was all caught on tape for them to memorialise. Paul moved on to his favourite kind of assault with that feat accomplished - brutal sex, particularly anal sex. Jane was so heavily drugged even the barbaric assault that Paul carried out on her couldn't wake her up.

After Paul was done, Karla cleaned the blood off the girl and put her to bed. The next day, Jane woke up sick and sore. Presuming it was all down to a night of heavy drinking, she had no clue what she'd really endured the night before. She was introduced to Paul on this day, too, believing it to be the first time they'd met.

Despite Karla's gift to Paul and his apparent gratitude for it, he was hesitant to go through with his upcoming marriage to her. He noticed she was ageing, she'd sped past her twenty-first birthday and she was far from the virgin he longed for. He was having second thoughts. Still, he went ahead with the extravagant wedding, perhaps not out of genuine love or even responsibility to Karla, but because it posed to be a financially lucrative event for him.

The lavish wedding bash took place at Niagara-on-the-Lake, complete with white horses pulling the carriage, copious amounts of champagne flowing and an expensive sit-down dinner where one hundred and fifty guests enjoyed plates of pheasant and all the trimmings. On the outside looking in, the loved-up couple were the embodiment of perfection, both attractive, successful and seemingly adored each other no end. In reality, the adoration was primarily one-sided.

Paul carefully orchestrated every minute detail of the wedding. From Karla's expensive wedding dress to the way she wore her hair to the flashy menu, Paul oversaw it all. The vows also had to adhere to his insistence of including Karla saying she'd "love, honour and obey" him in her vows. He didn't offer the same promise. He forbade the minister to call them "husband and wife." Paul declared they had to be called "man and wife."

For the luxurious event, Paul expected the guests to offer donations as wedding gifts. He worked out that, seeing as he was spending around fifty dollars per head, he'd expect they'd cough up about a hundred dollars each as a wedding gift. His goal was to make $50,000 off the back of his wedding to Karla.

Marriage wouldn't stifle the pair's lust for deviancy. In fact, Paul and Karla were only just beginning.

## The Descent Into Depravity

Leslie Mahaffy was what you might call rebellious. She had a strong, independent spirit that saw her breach the curfews imposed by her parents and skip class. She also went through a phase of shoplifting and was already sexually active despite her young age. Her despairing parents reacted by getting tough on young Leslie when she violated the rules they'd set out.

On June 14, 1991, Leslie headed out for the night with her group of friends, ending up staying out well past her curfew. At two in the morning, she eventually went back home, but sick of their daughter flouting the rules they'd set, the Mahaffy's locked Leslie out. With nowhere else to go, the teen called her friend to see if she could stay there until morning, but she said no on account of her mother not allowing friends over at such a late hour. Leslie said it was okay because she was headed back to her house to wake her parents up.

Leslie Mahaffy was never seen alive again.

Not daring to anger her parents by waking them, Leslie tried instead to see if she could get in the house without alerting her parents. In a twist of awful bad luck, the teen encountered Paul Bernardo as she loitered outside of her home. Paul wasn't actually looking for a girl to rape that night; he was out lurking in the darkness stealing licence plates. His new business venture saw him smuggling cigarettes from America, and he used these stolen plates to avoid rousing suspicion with his frequent trips across the border.

Seizing the sick opportunity, Paul pulled a knife out and forced Leslie into his car.

Paul did something he'd never done before - took one of the victims he'd attacked on the street back to his home. He did so without waking up Karla and bound 14-year-old Leslie so she couldn't move. He also blindfolded the terrified teen. When Karla did wake up, she was upset - because Paul had the audacity to use their best champagne glasses while torturing his new toy. Still, Karla knew she couldn't be upset for long; that would only push Paul away. She eventually came around and joined in on the abuse of Leslie Mahaffy.

Paul gave Karla precise and vulgar instructions on how he wanted her to sexually assault Leslie. He became the director of this sick film, barking orders at an obedient Karla to violate the teenager in disturbing and humiliating ways.

Every scene Paul shot had to be perfect. The film he was making was to be his personal cinematic masterpiece. After filming act one with Karla, Paul handed the directorial duties over to Karla as he forced himself on Leslie, who was crying in agony. Yet again, Paul carried out his violent ritual of brutal anal penetration on the teen. Her pleading only seemed to spur on the sick duo.

On the warm summer evening of June 29, 1991, a couple were out canoeing on Lake Gibson, enjoying the calm water as the sun was setting. However, their carefreeness was soon disrupted by their discovery of a concrete block with what appeared to be some chunks of animal skin folded in it. The man and his girlfriend swiftly left the water, but they couldn't forget what they saw. Unable to logically explain their find, the man went back to the spot where the ominous block was. Enlisting the help of a fisherman, the two men worked to pull out the heavy block of concrete so they could inspect it further. It seems the man just wanted to put his mind at ease, figuring there was some way to explain the odd flesh woven throughout the concrete. Looking at the block, the pair found a human foot.

It wasn't long before the lake was swarming with police, and they swiftly found four more concrete blocks in the water. The police come to the conclusion that whoever dumped these body-part filled blocks in Lake Gibson couldn't have been fa-

miliar with the area because they dumped the body in the shallow area of the water. If they'd known the area, surely they'd
have thrown the blocks off the bridge where the deep water
would've concealed their crime scene forever. With police
thoroughly searching the lake, a young woman's torso was
pulled from the water. The macabre finds made up a tragic jig-
saw puzzle; the torso matched up with the rest of the limbs that
were cut from it and encased in concrete. It was apparent the
body had been dismembered with a power saw. Leslie's brace
helped identify her.

After this, Paul felt deprived of the only form of entertainment
he enjoyed. This made him angry and miserable, which made
Karla panic that he was slipping from her clutches. She had to
do something, and fast.

In a fluster, she called Jane and lured her back into the fold.
Still, it wasn't an ideal situation; Jane wasn't exactly the virginal
sex slave Paul was after. At least, not since he stripped her virginity from her. She also rebuked Paul's advances, stating that
she didn't want to lose her virginity. This upset both Paul and
Karla. To pacify the couple, Jane did agree to some sexual contact with Paul, but this was a far cry from the sex slave he
yearned for.

Jane then confided in her riding instructor about the older man
and the sexual relations she was having with him. The instructor wasn't about to let the young girl be groomed and used and
quickly told Jane's mother.

This meant Paul and Karla had to be more covert about their abuse of the teenager. They pulled out their halothane soaked rag yet again and made sure Jane was none the wiser about Paul's horrific sexual violation of her. However, Karla and her history of using halothane that resulted in death looked to repeat itself; Jane stopped breathing as Karla was pressing the rag against her face during Paul's assault. The deviant pair raced to bring the teen back round and avoid her choking on her vomit like Tammy.

Luckily, their amateur attempts worked this time, and Jane began sputtering and coughing, but this didn't pacify a panicked Paul - he was full of blame and rage toward his wife. He questioned her capability of using halothane, he berated her for her uselessness, and he was incensed that yet again his homemade film was ruined. This made Karla frantic. Yet again, she had to do something to bring Paul back to her.

Teenager Terri Anderson disappeared on November 30, 1991. The vivacious young girl was full of life and her peppy attitude delighted Paul. Little has been released about Terri and her disappearance, but she vanished just over a mile from where Leslie Mahaffy was taken.

After this, the pair enlisted another young girl to help satisfy Paul's cravings, but she eventually moved to Ohio. This left the Bernardos lacking once again for excitement. These dips always caused tensions in the marriage and made Paul hostile and abusive towards Karla. She couldn't bear it.

In April 1992, a pretty and popular teenager was abducted from a parking lot. Karla had approached Kristen French and lured the young girl to her car under the pretence of being lost and needing the girl's help in getting directions. Happy to help, Kristen obliged and stood by the car and pointed at Karla's map, when suddenly Paul appeared out of nowhere and forced the afraid teenager into the backseat, threatening her with his knife.

Paul and Karla understood that Kristen had to die. She knew what they looked like. She knew where they lived. She had been in their house, knew the layout and even what kind of dog they had. She couldn't be set free, no matter what. Still, the pair were going to make use of the teen while they had her, and she wasn't to suspect that they were going to kill her when they were done.

Kristen cooperated with the sick pair and complied with their humiliating orders. She was a clever young girl and believed that in doing this, she would be able to survive and gain the trust of her captors. But as the hours turned to days, her ordeal became worse and more viscous. Paul became more sadistic. He told her he was going to urinate and defecate on her, which he did. He rubbed his groin on her face as he threatened to hurt her.

The flurry of indignities Kristen endured was - as usual - filmed for the future enjoyment of the Bernardos. The only thing the couple left off the video was Kristen's final indignity - her murder. By the end of that April, her naked body was found in a ditch. She hadn't been dismembered as Leslie had, causing investigators to wrongly assume the murders of the two teens were in no way connected.

Towards the end of the following month, Terri Anderson, who'd vanished the previous November, was found submerged in water at Port Dalhousie. There appeared to be no evidence of a crime, although it's difficult to determine such factors when a body has been immersed in water for half a year. Subsequently, the coroner ruled that although her death was by drowning, it was likely after drinking and taking LSD.

## The Investigation into the Scarborough Rapist

The police initially became aware of Paul Bernardo during his time as the dangerous and elusive Scarborough Rapist. A Toronto Metropolitan Police detective called Steve Irwin became heavily involved in this disturbing serial rape case, noting that there were too many similarities in the victims' stories for it to be more than one culprit. The descriptions were all similar, too. Victims told police of a well groomed young man with a pleasant smell and who had good teeth. As he assaulted his victims, he spoke all the while, telling the victim what he wanted to hear from them. All of the rapes occurred within a small radius in Scarborough's Guildwood Village.

Around the Christmas of 1987, one of the victims gave an incredibly specific description of her attacker. She described him as good looking, clean-shaven with no stubble, roughly six-foot, and having no visible tattoos. The description helped develop a composite picture of the attacker that resulted in an uncanny likeness to Paul Bernardo. Frustratingly, the police didn't publish the sketch right away.

Jennifer Galligan, one of Paul's ex-girlfriends, had already been to the police a number of times about him regarding his abuse towards her, including rape, assault and threats to harm her. Coincidences tied Paul to the rapes too: the attacker drove a white Ford Capri, as did Bernardo. He also lived in the same area the rapes happened. A subsequent report was filed, but nothing was done with it at the time.

It took until the May of 1990 before police released the sketch of the Scarborough Rapist, years after the attacks had begun. The victims had all had a say in the likeness of the picture, and they all agreed that the drawing was a true likeness of their attacker. This composite sketch, plus a hefty $150,000 reward for the identification of the rapist, caused a flurry of tips from the public. Some would be merely trying their luck at nabbing the money, others were more accurate in their suspicions of the rapist.

Paul was living solely on his cigarette-smuggling hustle by this point. However, his former colleagues from the accounting firm he worked at saw the picture in the papers, stunned at just how much it looked like Paul. Several people contacted the police and reported that the picture looked exactly like someone they knew - Paul Bernardo. Police were swamped with similar calls and had to choose which ones were followed up and looked into and which ones weren't. They didn't do anything with this information about Paul, which saw the rapist slip through the net of justice yet again.

Detective Irwin handed all of the physical evidence collected over the years from the rape victims and ensured that one person take responsibility for testing these crucial ties to the attacker. Kim Johnston was handed that task. She tested the semen samples and determined the rapist's blood type factors. She was also able to ascertain that the attacker was a non-secretor. These elements put him in a small percentage of the male population at just 12.8 per cent.

As the uncanny drawing was circulated, more and more of Paul's former colleagues and acquaintances contacted police about the startling resemblance the drawing was of him. Detective Irwin had no choice but to pay Bernardo a visit since the calls about him matching the sketch were coming in too thick and fast to ignore. Paul, ever the articulate, engaging and seemingly decent young man, didn't strike the detective as the type of person to be a serial rapist, as if these criminals have some kind of tick that would give their perversions away. Still, Detective Irwin took blood, hair, and saliva samples as a precaution.

These samples, along with hundreds of samples from other men fitting the rapist's description, were passed to Kim Johnston. She worked through the samples, eventually finding that just 5 out of the 230 total samples matched the blood factors of the Scarborough rapist. Among those five was Paul Bernardo. His

DNA was sent for some more testing in the spring of 1992. However, by this point, the elusive rapist had suddenly stopped his brutal attacks, causing the case to lose its sense of urgency.

The samples containing the identity of the attacker were put on the shelf for the time being.

The Benardo's were living (and killing) in St. Catharine's by now, and the police were primarily investigating the Niagara Falls area. Vince Bevan headed the case after the body of Leslie Mahaffy was uncovered. After the murder of Kristen French, the Green Ribbon Task Force was formed by the Ontario government. The hub of operations was set up on the outskirts of St. Catherine's. The force was aided by the American FBI.

When Kristen French was snatched, a witness recalled seeing a tussle happening in a car at the scene of the abduction. She wasn't familiar with the names or makes of cars, but she thought the kidnapper's car was a Camaro. With this new information, Vince Bevan tracked the owners of all the Camaro in the area.

At the same time, Bernardo's name was again rising to the surface; the tips were flowing in at an incredibly rapid pace. Of the back of this, a couple of police officers eventually called in on Paul at the Bayview property. Ever the charmer, Paul was incredibly polite, well-spoken and accommodating when talking to the officers, even admitting that he was aware he'd been a suspect in the rapes due to the similarities he bore to the police sketch. Upon speaking to Paul, the two officials interviewing him noted that he was incredibly clean-cut, and kept a very clean and orderly house. Plus, looking outside, they could see he drove a Nissan, not a Camaro. In fact, the two vehicles looked nothing alike.

Still, Paul wasn't off the hook just yet. The final DNA samples had yet to be done. While Detective Irwin sent the Green Ribbon Task Force some helpful information, he neglected to send over interviews of those close to Paul who'd tipped the police off about him. He also didn't send over a report from a woman that claimed Bernardo was stalking her. There were also damning reports filed by his ex-girlfriend, Jennifer Galligan, that weren't passed over. Therefore, Paul Bernardo was not viewed as a real suspect and wasn't pursued for the rapes.

Finally, in early 1993, several years after blood samples had been taken from Paul Bernardo, the forensic lab in Toronto eventually analysed his blood. There was now irrefutable evidence - Paul had raped the victims from whom they'd managed to collect semen samples. The frustrating reality is that if the laboratory had been quicker in their testing, Paul wouldn't have been able to rape more young girls - he'd have been in jail.

Detective Irwin ensured that Paul was put under complete surveillance. Upon doing this, he learned that he'd just been charged with assaulting his wife in St. Catharine's.

**Karla - Callous Killer Or Victim?**

Paul counted on having full control of Karla, regardless of how poorly he treated her. So much so, he began ramping up his abuse of her in the summer of '92, believing that he could beat her up horrifically and she'd still stick by his side. This was true

- to a point. When it came to asking her to do vile, cruel and abhorrent things to others, it seems Karla didn't see these things as dealbreakers. However, it seemed like being beaten up wasn't something she'd tolerate for as long. It may have taken numerous black eyes, horrific facial bruising, and enduring beatings with various household implements, but Karla found it in her to leave Paul. One particular beating was worse than the rest; the abuse was so torturous and relentless Karla couldn't shrug it off as an accident as she had all those times before. Her work colleagues contacted her parents, and they begged her to leave Paul. It was now January 1993, and Karla sought refuge in the home of her surviving sister's friend. It turns out this woman's husband was a Toronto policeman.

The Niagara police were subsequently called and got Karla the medical treatment she needed.

The following month, with the investigation of Paul broadening, the Ontario Green Ribbon Task Force and the Toronto police wanted to speak with Karla urgently. They wanted her fingerprints and to talk to her about a unique Mickey Mouse watch she had - one that was very much the same as Kristen French's watch.

Detectives in Toronto interviewed Karla for hours. Karla wasn't stupid - she knew the police had tied the Scarborough rapist to the killings in the St. Catherines area from the types of questions they were asking. Karla was panicked by the interrogation, knowing the net was closing in. She decided to tell her uncle that she knew who the serial rapist was. Not only that, she also knew who murdered Kristen French and Leslie Mahaffy; it was her abusive husband, Paul.

In anticipation of the impending fallout, Karla quickly got a top lawyer.

During her time working in a veterinary clinic, Karla met lawyer George Walker when she took care of his sick Dalmatian. After many conversations and interviews with Karla, George came to suspect that she perhaps wasn't just another innocent victim of the abusive rapist and killer. Despite painting herself this way, he wasn't sure she wasn't a big part of Paul's deviant lifestyle. He wasn't sure what her role was in these sick crimes, but he had a niggling feeling she definitely played a part. With these doubts in mind, he had to consider what he could do to gain her full cooperation in the case.

That February, Paul was finally arrested in relation to the Scarborough rapes as well the Mahaffy and French murders. Karla wasn't shocked - she knew this was coming. But she was engulfed with fear. Fear of Paul. Fear of the consequences. Fear of her life being taken away from her. Fearful of the truth coming out. During this time, she tried to quell her anxieties with pills and alcohol.

In mid-February, police obtained and executed search warrants for the Bernardos home. There was a library of videotapes stacked with pornography, depraved sexual acts caught on camera and an abundance of serial killer videos. There was also a book of written descriptions of each attack the Scarborough

Rapist had carried out. Police also discovered a short home-made video that showed Karla engaging in sex acts with two women, enthusiastic and confidently, perhaps showing that she wasn't as coerced by Paul as she'd made out.

The following week, George Walker discussed the case with Murray Segal, a specialist in plea bargains. George was looking into what deals he could get for Karla. It was understood Karla would get a total of twelve years behind bars for each of the two young victims, although the sentences would be served concurrently. This meant parole would be a possibility in three years, proving her behaviour was reasonable.

The Canadian government agreed to speak to the parole board on behalf of Karla, stressing the significance of her damning testimony against Paul. Murray agreed to do whatever he had to for Karla to serve out the sentence in a psychiatric hospital instead of being sent to jail. The upcoming trial, it was discussed, would be short - a formality - and Karla would waive her right to a preliminary hearing. However, this leniency came at a price; Karla would need to tell the complete truth about Paul and her involvement in the things he did. She would need to confess, 100% transparency, to everything she and Paul did. Karla agreed.

By now it was early March, and Karla was sent to a psychiatric unit for assessment. During this stint, she was prescribed heavy doses of sedatives, insisting that her dose be upped. It was here she sat down and wrote a letter to her parents and little sister. The letter was short and to the point, with words of sorrow and sadness but no real remorse exhibited. She confesses to murdering Tammy, telling her parents that Paul was in love with Tammy and wanted to rape her. She says that she can't make them understand what Paul put her through and she was "stupid" to go through with the depraved plans. When talking about Tammy's final moments, she says she's unsure if it was the copious amount of drugs she fed her or the food she ate that night that made her vomit. She ends the letter by saying if she could trade places with Tammy, she would.

## The Trial Begins...

Kicking off in June 1993, the trial had become something of a media frenzy. People were outraged, shocked, angry, and Karla was vilified. The Canadian public eagerly followed the trail, hoping for justice to well and truly be served.

The psychiatric report that had been compiled during her time in the hospital set the stage for the (now infamous) plea bargain deal. Dr Malcolm, who spent hours talking to Karla and assessing her, concluded that while she knew what Paul was doing, she was helpless to intervene for fear of her own safety. He said that her lack of defence for the victims - or even herself - was because she'd become so unquestionably obedient and subservient to Paul that the idea of standing up to him paralysed her with fear.

Rightly anticipating public outcry over the lenient plea bargain, Murray Segal had a few words to try to combat the backlash. Speaking of Karla, he said, "Without her, the true state of affairs might never be known." He argued that a guilty plea is the traditional hallmark of remorse, emphasising her age, lack

of criminal record, and abuse suffered at the hands of her hus
band and her somewhat secondary role in the murders were
factors. He stressed she was unlikely to re-offend.

Karla received the previously agreed sentence of 12 years, bu
it wasn't over for her yet. She still had to prepare herself for the
upcoming trial of Paul Bernardo - and he had evidence for the
court that would certainly show her in a much different light.

Paul's trial didn't take place for two years after his arrest. A big
reason for the lengthy delay was that Paul had put his lawyer
Ken Murray, in a tough ethical dilemma. He'd handed Ken
the damning videotapes of him and Karla raping and torturing
their victims. He thought by directing his lawyer to the hidden
incriminating tapes, they'd never be seen by the prosecution.

There was a problem, though; prosecutors were aware of the ex
istence of the tapes. They wiretapped Paul's conversations with
his lawyer hoping they'd trip up and discuss the homemade
films. Pressure mounted on Ken to do something with the
videotapes he was keeping secret. It was eventually too much
for the lawyer to be burdened with and he turned them over to
the prosecutors before removing himself from the case. Estab
lished defence lawyer John Rosen then stepped up to represent
Paul.

By the time May 1995 rolled around, Paul's trial had finally be
gun. The videotapes were shown as damning pieces of evidence
against the killer. Paul was facing two counts of first-degree
murder, two of sexual assault, kidnapping, and another count
of carrying out an act of indignity on a dead body.

The public hasn't been aware of the true magnitude of Karla's involvement in the heinous crimes, seeing as her trial (which took place almost two years earlier) didn't expose the extent of her sexual degradation and seeming lust for brutality and murder. The prosecution started with a clip that showed Karla completely naked in front of the camera, excitedly playing up for the homemade movie. The courtroom was full of gasps, people both shocked and disgusted as Karla touched herself as Paul filmed.

After the videos were shown, it was explained that the dialogue used by Karla in the clips had been clearly scripted by a demanding and controlling Paul. It was noted that these videos show just how much he was able to force his desires on Karla.

The recording was blatantly geared to sexually excite the director, Paul. Karla talked of acquiring young virgins for him to rape. The entirety of her words spoken was a mishmash of Paul's sexual fantasies with the aim of the whole video was to please him. Karla was the slave, Paul was "The King", as he liked to be called. More videotapes were shown. Leslie, Kristen and Jane Doe were all caught on film. They were tortured, beaten, raped and degraded for all to see. There could be little doubt about Paul's horrific depravity now.

There was more to come. Karla was eventually called to the stand after the videos were shown and was asked to explain and elaborate on what the jurors had just witnessed.

She described her relationship with Paul as one filled with sexual degradation - extremely similar to what Paul had done to other girlfriends before Karla. When he met Karla, who became his willing victim, his degradation escalated until there was no such thing as boundaries. He forced her to wear a dog's choke chain. He cruelly inserted a bottle into her vagina. During one rape, he almost strangled Karla to death with a wire cord. Paul explained to Karla that his fantasy of choking her wouldn't hurt her. The abuse was also verbal and name-calling was a daily occurrence. He said she was a slut who no one else would ever want.

When the defence took the floor in the courtroom, they immediately attacked Karla's credibility as a witness. They claimed she wasn't the helpless victim she tried to portray herself as, but rather a willing and eager participant in the rape and murder spree the couple embarked on.

Despite Paul's see-through narcissism and sheer depravity, he was at least able to expose Karla as being a morally bankrupt, remorseless woman. It was Kristen's murder that served to expose just how heartless and devoid of empathy she was; the killer pair decided she had to die so they could spend Easter with Karla's family. Straight after Kristen was strangled to death - by either of the Bernardos, since they blamed each other - Karla went and blow-dried her damp hair. It was becoming clear that Karla had cleverly manipulated the justice system to develop one of the arguably worst plea bargains that the Canadian government has ever offered a criminal.

In September of 1995, Paul Bernardo was finally convicted of all the charges brought against him; all of the kidnappings, violent rapes and the horrific murders of Leslie Mahaffy and Kristen French.

On July 4, 2005, Karla was released from prison after serving the agreed-upon sentence. She's gone on to remarry and has three children, things her victims will never be able to do.

# Nannie Doss

The crimes of Nannie Doss are as baffling as they are heartless, and despite her relatively high body count, her crimes aren't as prolific or covered in the media as much as other female serial killers. Initially learning about her crimes from a documentary (that I can no longer find, even on the internet, although there are quite a few newer documentaries that retell her story), I was struck by just how callous this woman was. The motive for the crimes she committed was sorely lacking; she just didn't have one, which makes this case all the more absurd.

Her name, 'Nannie Doss', conjures up images of a sweet, older woman, one who perhaps dotes on her grandchildren and cooks hearty meals for her family. It certainly doesn't correlate with the despicable acts she carried out repeatedly. Underneath the pleasant and likeable facade was a woman you'd never want to cross paths with if you knew just how easy she found it to snuff out the life of another.

Nannie was a serial killer who murdered those closest to her. From the 1920s to the mid-50s, she was on a killing spree, mercilessly ending the lives of four of her husbands, moving from state to state as she did so. When she was eventually arrested for her crimes, she let out a chuckle. This wasn't a one-off incident brought on by nerves or a defence mechanism, either; Nannie continued to chuckle throughout the subsequent police interrogation, letting out giggles as she named the unsuspecting husbands she'd snuffed out.

Because of this peculiar behaviour, the press gave her the moniker "The Giggling Granny." Some dubbed her "The Jolly Widow." She laughed her way through all police interviews and we can only speculate why that was. Perhaps she really did find it funny how she'd killed her husbands - by using prunes of all things - or perhaps it was a giggle of embarrassment at being caught. Maybe she was trying to stifle the cruel, heartless side of her. What can be ascertained, however, is that she showed no remorse for the heinous crimes she committed.

Born Nancy Hazle to poor farmworkers in Blue Mountain, Nannie (as she would later prefer to be called) grew up with a love for romance magazines. The idea of romance enthralled her and took her away to a wonderland filled with happy endings and encounters with her knight in shining armour. Her love for these magazines framed her ideology of relationships and none of her future partners would ever live up to the perfection of those written about in romance magazines.

Nannie certainly travelled as she got older. She killed her husbands in Alabama, North Carolina, Oklahoma, and Kansas. There are other suspected victims as well. Nannie is also believed to have killed her mother, as well as two out of her four daughters. She's also alleged to have murdered a mother-in-law and other in-laws, usually by her preferred form of murder: feeding them prunes peppered with rat arsenic. Undoubtedly not your typical granny.

As a youngster, Nancy Hazle's life offered little in common to the romance magazines she loved so much. Enchantment and love weren't a part of her life, but that wouldn't stop her from spending a lifetime in search of it.

Her mother, Lou, offered Nancy all the care and comfort she could, but she was undeniably fearful of her poor-tempered husband, James Hazle. As a result, Nancy's life growing up wasn't a happy one. As she arrived at school age, she would start to go by the name Nannie, although school wasn't something she regularly attended, albeit through no fault of her own - if daddy wanted the kids to stay home and help on the farm, that's what they did. Nannie eventually had three sisters and a brother to keep her company when doing labour on the farm, although none of the siblings could protect one another from James Hazle's rageful beatings.

At five, Nannie was out ploughing fields, chopping wood as best she could, and undertaking heavy-lifting tasks like moving debris from the land. Games and playing with friends were strictly prohibited. While school may have been some kind of respite for young Nannie, it was still an arduous task - it was a four-mile round trip on foot.

Nannie's life was stripped of fun. If she stayed up past her bedtime, it wasn't to partake in family fun or enjoy time with her parents; it was to finish cleaning the dirty dishes and clean the home. Still, a late-night wasn't an excuse for a lie-in. Before the sun could rise, it was time to get up. Daddy would chastise his children out of their pit, hurrying them to the fields.

Growing up in this kind of suppressive environment, Nannie escaped reality by dreaming of finding love. Her sole interest was reading her mother's stack of romance publications, spending hours curled up in her bedroom and allowing those magazines to take her away from her mundane life. Her favourite part to devour was the lonely hearts section.

The early 1900s saw every young female want to look like a Gibson Girl, which was seen as the pinnacle of female attractiveness. This meant donning tight corsets, having a perfect hourglass figure and wearing statement bouffant hair piled up neatly atop the head. Despite her father's strictness, Nannie was no different; she wanted to look attractive to be wanted by the Prince Charmings she'd spent so long reading about.

As she arrived at dating age, her father stepped in immediately to veto any ideas she had about courting. James Hazle viewed Nannie and her siblings as free field hands, and he wasn't going to give up that kind of labour without a fight. The girls weren't allowed to go to the church socials, and Saturday gatherings at the local tavern were forbidden too. Wearing makeup was out of the question as far as father Hazle was concerned, as were silk stockings, fitted dresses and fixed up hair-dos. He made sure his daughters knew they wouldn't be tempting any male without his blessing. In fact, when daddy decided the time was right, he would be the one to pick his daughter's suitors.

While other teens were out socialising and even going on dates, weekend evenings found the Hazle sisters sat sorrowfully at home. From their house, they could see the bright lights of the barn just down the road, where a loud dance was taking place.

Daddy Hazle had made sure the closest they got to that gathering was behind the confines of their bedroom window. The girls could hear the gleeful yelling at the dance as they stared out at the plethora of other youths enjoying themselves.

Nannie had a rebellious streak, however. She sometimes managed to sneak away and take boys back to the hayloft. She only ever had a small window of time to make the events in the romance magazines a reality, so she seized these opportunities when she could. As long as her dad never found out, Nannie saw no reason not to partake in these midnight escapades. The boys certainly seemed to like her; she made herself easily available to them.

Nannie's mother could well have been aware of her daughter's nighttime activities but never drew attention to it. It could be that she partly wanted her child to get pregnant, which would have allowed her to flee the dictatorship she was under with James Hazle.

However, something very different happened; Hazle found out about Nannie's fling with young Charley Braggs and gave it his seal of approval. Charley was Nannie's co-worker at the Linen Thread Company, and he pursued the 16-year-old, which made her think of the stories from her romance magazines. Charley was tall, good-looking with a mop of curly hair. James Hazle thought that this young boy was different from the other Blue Mountain youngsters who frittered their time away at parties and the like. Charley was out there earning money, which was a huge plus in father Hazle's eyes. His earnings helped support his poorly mother, which was another tick for Nannie's dad - this boy had respect for his elders, he thought. Maybe wayward Nannie could learn a thing or two from this boy.

Charley Braggs was hugely successful in winning James over, and this meant one thing: the young pair would need to get married. Whether Nannie wanted it or she didn't. Four months after Charley met his future father-in-law, he married teenage Nannie.

Nannie would later write about the event, and it was clear she was hesitant about the whole affair. She noted she only married because her father insisted. She also wrote about how hesitant she was to marry a man who she'd only known a short while and who had an overbearing mother.

Nannie hadn't managed to shake off her demanding father; instead, she'd traded him for an equally as demanding mother-in-law. Should Nannie request to eat out at a restaurant, mother Braggs would have to come along. If she didn't want her son and her new daughter-in-law to go out, she would feign illness and make her doting son stay in and take care of her.

Within a four-year period, the couple had four children. The first was born in 1923 and the last in 1927. With raising four babies, trying hard to please the ever-demanding Mother Braggs, keeping a tidy house and forever cooking for a perpetually hungry husband, Nannie sought solace in the liquor cupboard. She also developed a chronic smoking habit. When these vices no longer helped her escape her domestic purgatory, she sought out strangers to take her away from her drab reality.

She headed to Blue Mountain's various gin mills, where she knew she could find drunk patrons to paw at her and fluff up her sense of worth. She needed to feel attractive, and this was the only way she saw how. Her infidelity and absence from the family home managed to go unnoticed as Charley was himself often inebriated or partaking in his own extramarital affairs. If the couple did end up spending any time together, it was purely accidental.

Tragedy would strike in early 1927 when Nannie and Charley's two middle daughters suddenly died due to suspected food poisoning. Both youngsters seemed perfectly fine sitting at the breakfast table but would be dead by midday. The medics who arrived at the scene recorded the premature deaths as accidental. Not everyone was convinced that this was right, especially Charley Braggs. He had no real proof, just a gut feeling that his wife was sinister and heartless enough to do something so dreadful, causing him to flee with his eldest daughter. He left the newborn behind.

While there is no physical proof that Nannie cruelly slayed her kids, there is little room for doubt that she cruelly snuffed them out - particularly when the method of murder used is one she would utilise time and time again on her unsuspecting lovers. But why would she do this to two of her children? It could be that she was perhaps overwhelmed with the stresses and responsibility of being a mother and wife, struggling to feed those two extra mouths. Maybe, it was a cold-hearted matter of economics.

Charley Braggs was undoubtedly frightened of his wife and her undeniable mean streak. So was his mother. He was wary enough of Nannie to never, ever drink or eat anything she should offer him when she was in a bad mood.

When Charley up and left with his eldest, it wasn't for a couple of days, as was the norm. He vanished without a word for months. His beloved mother had passed away during this time too, as he kept a solid distance between himself and his menacing wife. While Charley knew of his wife's sinister side, if he brought this up to outsiders, he knew they'd laugh or not take him seriously. Nannie was the picture of domesticity on the outside, and nobody would believe she was capable of murder. With her husband abandoning the family home, perhaps never to return, Nannie was in need of some cash. She took a job at the closest cotton mill to support herself.

Towards the end of summer 1928, Charley returned to Blue Mountain, an entire year after he fled his wife. He didn't come back alone. He brought his daughter, Melvina, and another woman and her child. Surprisingly, barely any words were exchanged between the trio of adults, and Nannie calmly took the hint. She packed her things up, took her daughters, and left, all the while cursing Charley under her breath. If Charley hadn't returned with a girlfriend in tow, who knows what the consequences could have been. Charley didn't know it, but he was the husband who got away. The rest wouldn't be so lucky.

**Husband Number Two: Frank**

After the marriage to Charley Briggs broke down, Nannie began working in a cotton mill on the outskirts of Blue Mountain. Days there were long, and the conditions were hot, but it got her out of the house. Now more than ever, escaping the confines of a house filled with responsibility was imperative. She'd moved back in with her parents, who nagged and berated Nannie, although they offered her the childcare she wanted. This allowed the young woman to take off and do as she pleased.

Still, she wasn't going to make the same mistake twice. She wouldn't be marrying an immature boy with an overbearing mother. Nor would she put up with wandering eyes, despite the fact that she would frequently partake in extramarital affairs while with Charley. Nannie turned to a great source of comfort through her childhood to seek out a new partner - the lonely hearts column. She wrote to men whose adverts she found intriguing. Out of all the responses, one particularly piqued her attention - Frank Harrelson, who was 23 and, judging from his enclosed picture, looked just like Clark Gable. She responded with a picture of her own and a cake she baked especially for him.

The letters got steamier, filled with suggestive prose and double entendres.

Frank lived close in nearby Jacksonville, and after some back and forth, he eventually got in his beat-up old car and raced south to Blue Mountain to meet his dream girl. He arrived at her house, anxiously waiting at the door to meet Nannie in person. When she answered, he was pleasantly surprised. Her picture didn't do her justice. Her picture had also failed to capture her eyes adequately. They were almost black, which only served to add a sense of mystery to the young woman.

He quickly proposed, and she swiftly accepted. By 1929 they were married. The honeymoon period lasted through autumn and winter, where the couple were happily loved up. All the while, Frank would binge on alcohol, which wasn't an issue for Nannie initially. However, it soon transpired that her good-looking husband was also an alcoholic. Not only that, he exposed himself as a violent one at that, even serving time in jail for assault.

When she married Frank, Nannie had picked up her daughters from Grandma Hazle's loving home - a place the two young girls had grown used to and enjoyed being - and brought them to Jacksonville with her. The youngsters were in for a shock when they met their new stepfather; he was argumentative, aggressive and drunk more often than not. The girls became used to the cops showing up at the house every week to inform Nannie that her husband was in jail yet again for drunken behaviour. The sisters saw their mothers dark moods grow more intense, her actions becoming somehow sinister, particularly when she would drag a slurring Frank back home from the cells.

Life remained this way for a long time. Despite her resentment towards her big disappointment of a husband, Nannie tolerated him for many years. Frank's drinking barely ever let up, and he wasn't averse to smacking her around should his drunkenness turn to rage. He'd scream and yell threats at her and her daughters for the sixteen years they were married. Perhaps it wasn't love or sympathy that stopped Nannie from ending the marriage - or her husband - sooner. It could just be that she'd not yet found the courage to end the life of an adult who could possibly fight back. Killing her daughters was easy; a necessity for her to be able to carry on with life. How could she snuff out a big, strapping man anyway? Nannie wasn't far away from answering that macabre question that often burned in the back of her mind, particularly when she was left with a black eye or injured feelings.

By the early 40s, her surviving daughters had grown up and got married. Her eldest, Melvina, gave birth to Robert in 1943, and by 1945, she went into labour with her second child. The small-framed woman struggled with this pregnancy, afraid of giving birth again and dealing with agonising pains this time, she asked mother Nannie to be by her side. Nannie stayed with her daughter throughout the night, wiping away the beads of sweat on her forehead and comforting the exhausted young woman through the ordeal. The matriarch also ordered Melvina's husband around, telling him to bring water, towels, blankets and to make sure the nurses were aware of the pregnant woman's needs. You couldn't argue that Nannie was being a doting mother, and when her granddaughter was finally born, she stepped into the role of adoring grandmother immediately.

The child was dead within an hour of being born.

Details after this are a bit foggy. The newborn baby girl had fallen asleep in the hospital room and exhausted mother Melvina, drifting in and out of a post-birth haze, lay in bed next to her. At some point, she happened to turn and face her mother as she was holding the baby in her arms. But, this wasn't a loving kind of hold; Melvina saw Nannie sticking a hatpin into the newborn's head. She couldn't work out if she really saw this or it was part of a surreal nightmare.

This understandably bothered a distraught Melvina, even more so after the doctors were unable to give a reason for the child's premature death. When she returned home a few days later, Melvina quietly and nervously told her husband and her sister about what she thought she had witnessed Nannie doing to the baby. Safe to say, her family were startled at the revelation, although it did help them remember something that had been innocent enough at the time; they recall how granny Nannie was constantly playing with said hatpin earlier that night, intertwining it between her fingers.

Six months passed before another tragedy struck. Melvina was enduring heartache after heartache when her son Robert also suddenly passed away. He was being taken care of by Nannie when he sadly died. Melvina was staying with her father, Charley, after a particularly heated fight with her husband. This left little Robert in the care of his grandmother. Exactly how little Robert died was a mystery, but doctors would record his death as "asphyxia" from causes unknown. Doting grandmother Nannie appeared to be heartbroken by the loss and wailed as she lowered his tiny coffin into his grave. The grief-stricken act at his funeral included fainting and shrieking. It only took her a few months to go ahead and collect the $500 life insurance check she'd recently taken out on the child.

Her killing skills were now proving to be refined enough to avoid detection and any suspicion from outsiders. The theatrics she could put on display after the deaths only further propelled her belief that she could kill and never be thought of as being the culprit. Babies, she found, were easy to kill. Now she was ready to tackle a bigger target: her drunken, abusive, and all-around disappointment of a husband, Frank Harrelson. She awaited the opportunity to strike, but even a cold-hearted killer like Nannie felt she needed a little provocation before she ended his life. She didn't need to wait long before Frank lashed out at her, triggering Nannie's lust for death.

## Nannie Discovers Her Modus Operandi

America had been plunged into a world war; GIs who were sent to Europe were dying at a rapid pace, and with such horrifying things happening in a chaotic world, the deaths of a newborn girl and a toddler in the foothills of Alabama weren't looked into as much as the possibly otherwise would have been. However, by August 1945, the remaining enemy, Japan, surrendered, and the joyful nation only had one thing on their minds: welcoming home their sons, brothers, and fathers. Every state was covered in an abundance of bunting, flags and balloons; Alabama was certainly no exception. As the sun went down on September 15, 1945, an ecstatic Frank Harrelson headed over to the local tavern to welcome home his friends who'd just come back from overseas. While he didn't need an excuse to get drunk on this night, or any night, patriotism had given him a hall pass to really get intoxicated.

He was still in good spirits when he arrived home late that night. He wanted sex, but Nannie declined. He wasn't taking no for an answer and punched his ham-like hand into the wall, threatening Nannie with not only violence but also his departure if she didn't comply. To avoid more black eyes or a busted lip, Nannie gave into brutish Frank's demands. He climbed on top of his incensed wife as she stared at the ceiling, silently plotting her revenge.

The following day, while tending to her much-loved rose garden, Nannie found Frank's liquor jar hidden in the nearby flowerbed. Coupled with the events that happened the night before, enough was enough for Nannie. She always kept a pretty garden, and she would not let that man ruin it with his filthy secret jars of booze. She stormed to the storeroom with the jar in hand, poured away a good amount of his bitter concoction, only to top it up with one of her own - rat poison. Frank wasn't going to leave his jar of liquor left alone for too long, and Nannie knew this. He died that evening in excruciating agony. He was thirty-eight. While her husband's body was still warm, Nannie took the empty jar from where it laid and washed it.

Nannie was now free to do as she wished. No longer tied down by an abusive husband, she hit the road. Travelling all over by rail, to New York and then Idaho, it's anyone's guess exactly what she did during this period. This portion of her life is largely unaccounted for, although there is some evidence she may have married again to someone with the surname Hendrix. Whatever happened to him is unknown, but knowing what we know now about Nannie, it's likely we can take a good guess.

Wherever she roamed after becoming a widow, nowhere was deemed good enough to call home until she wound up in the small picturesque town of Lexington, North Carolina. She headed here to chase a lonely-hearts lead named Arlie Lanning. They met for the first time here, marrying two days later. There were lots of things Nannie was not, one of them being a time-waster.

Her new life with Arlie wasn't nearly as chaotic or dramatic as it was with Frank, possibly due to the fact that Nannie often wasn't home with him. Whenever things got too much, when Arlie consumed too much liquor, when he strayed too far away with another woman, Nannie packed her bags and took off. Arlie, like his predecessor, was a drunk who loved the company of women, but unlike Frank, he wasn't violent. Still, there were things that Nannie wouldn't abide by, and she would take off for months at a time, letting her spouse know she was gone with a blunt note shoved under a jar saying "GONE." She would get in touch occasionally while on her jaunts, asking for money or just to let her husband know she'd be back at some point.

When she did come back to the marital home, Arlie would shrug a greeting her way, but that was it. Sometimes when she came back, he was in no fit state to even acknowledge her as he'd be unconscious from drinking too much. Then, in fits and starts, the pair would play the adoring couple. After Nannie blamed Arlie's drinking and womanising on her departures, he would - for a short while at least - commit to going cold turkey on both. They both knew, however, this would only last days or weeks before the bad behaviour would return.

When she was at home, Nannie portrayed herself as the perfect wife. This was only for the benefit of the locals and neighbours, though. Her frequent jaunts away would be explained away as her visiting friends or family. Sometimes, this wasn't a lie; Nannie would occasionally take the bus to Gadsden, Alabama, to take care of her cancer-stricken sister Dovie. Still, the Lexington locals all saw Nannie as a doting wife and thoroughly domestic woman. She often had sweet apple pies cooling at the window, and her laundry would fill the air with the fresh scent of citrus. Her garden, her pride and joy, was tended to with love and care, leading up to what appeared to be a well-kept house. Still, domesticity wasn't what Nannie craved. She still read her romance magazines, and the handsome heroes in those publications weren't anything like her real-life romances. Still, Nannie wasn't overly literate and sometimes struggled to grasp what she was reading if the writing was a little complex. That issue would soon be resolved with a new modern-day invention: the television.

Nannie loved watching teleplays and stand-up comedy shows, but when a love story came on, that was Nannie's idea of heaven. She'd pile up a plate full of dinner leftovers, open up a pack of Camel cigarettes, line up the ashtray beside her and collapse into the comfortable armchair reserved for moments like this. The black and white screen would flicker a tale of lust, love and heartthrobs.

Nannie was a frequent churchgoer in Lexington and, as a result, had become close with not only the minister's family but also many of the families in the congregation. Arlie, should he be sober enough, would go with his wife to the Sunday morning services and the follow-up gatherings for tea or picnics. However, there were plenty of whispers among the group about Arlie. His reputation preceded him. Before - as well as during - his union with Nannie, he was frequently spotted in the area of lower Lexington where the "floozies flocked." He would invariably be draped over one of those floozies. Arlie was a known scoundrel among the people of the Lexington Church, and the community felt for poor Nannie. They didn't know if she was clued up about his wandering eye, but they didn't want to be the one to burst her bubble. Behind closed doors in quiet conversation, Arlie became the town's villain, with families scolding him in hushed conversations behind closed doors. Nannie, on the other hand, became the town's saint.

It came as a bit of a surprise, then, when Arlie died, just how many people turned up to the funeral. The whole town made it to pay their respects at the burial in February 1950, but not for the man in the coffin, but for his grieving wife, Nannie. Arlie's death was sudden and unexpected. Heart failure was the cause, according to the doctor.

Naturally, something had caused young Arlie's heart to fail, but the doctor felt no need to be suspicious of the relatively young man's death. An autopsy would be a waste of resources when there was no foul play detected. Numerous underlying ailments could have caused him the horrific attack of pain he endured before his death. After all, there was a deadly strain of flu virus currently sweeping Alabama, and like most viruses, it affects some worse than others. He exhibited all of the typical symptoms - profuse sweating, projectile vomiting, dizziness. Add to the fact that Arlie wasn't in the best of shape due to his alcohol consumption, the doctor was confident in his cause of death.

Nannie was convincing in her explanation of his death, too. She was noted as saying Arlie simply sat down that fateful morning, drank his usual cup of coffee and ate the bowl of pre-prepared prunes Nannie had given him, as was the norm. Nannie insists he looked in a fine state until that afternoon. A mere two days later, her husband was dead. His widow would sob at his funeral how she nursed him - she really did her best to get him better - but she failed. Dabbing her watery eyes, she described that his last words told of the true cause of his death; Arlie told Nannie that the coffee did this to him.

## The Widow Grieves... But Not For Long

Two months after Arlie's sudden passing, the home that he shared with Nannie had burned to the ground. Luck was on the widow's side that day, not only because had the house survived the fire, it would have gone to his sister (as per his will). Luck also saw that Nannie was not home as the fire blazed, as she'd just left the property with her pride and joy, the TV strapped into the back seat of her truck. She was, she insisted, on the way to get the thing repaired. Subsequently, the insurance people issued a check to Arlie Lanning, which found its way to Arlie's mother's house, where Nannie was now staying. Almost as soon as the check arrived, Nannie rushed to cash it in. Shortly after this, Arlie's mother died suddenly in her sleep, but Nannie was already on her way to North Carolina.

She arrived on her sister's doorstep, TV under her arm, where she said she was going to take care of her poorly sibling. Dovie wouldn't last much longer under Nannie's care; she died that summer, in her sleep. Coupled with Nannie's dark, sinister side was a self-serving intelligence. While she killed wherever she went, she always made sure there was a benefit to it for her, whether that be money, sympathy or a fresh start. In this case, it was all three.

For a $15 per annum fee, people seeking life partners could join The Diamond Circle Club. Members seeking suitors received a monthly newsletter covering the newest members and disclosing their desires in a partner. Nannie, of course, was intrigued. The year was 1952, and the serial murderer was at it again.

By this point, Nannie had put on a significant amount of weight. She wore glasses permanently, and her once-svelte profile was now masked by a double chin and jowls. She didn't turn heads like she used to, and this fact wasn't lost on Nannie. So, she decided, it was time to seek out a different kind of mate. Someone mature, someone who boasted personality instead of looks. A real man, she thought. And it didn't take long for her to come across one - former businessman Richard Morton from Kansas.

At 47, Nannie's hair was slightly greying, her hips were wider, and her skin wasn't quite as dewy as it once had been. Still, she had that girlish giggle that didn't fail to win over whichever man she chose. Her mysterious glistening eyes, her flirtatious flattery and engaging glances were all still intact.

Richard, now retired, wanted change and excitement in his life. He found that in Nannie, and after a short while, he wrote to Diamond Circle, requesting to be deleted from the member's list and thanked them for introducing him to the most "wonderful woman I have ever met." By October 1952, they were married, and Nannie and her TV moved into his humble property in Emporia.

The flat plains of Kansas were a stark contrast to the vast mountains and ample greenery Nannie was used to. For a time, the sunset on the surrounding horizon enchanted her. She even felt a surge of happiness in the arms of her husband, perhaps even contentment. Richard was half American Indian, over 6-feet tall, with dark features, apart from his piercing eyes - he looked just like the romance magazines described. He also treated her well, bought her whatever she wanted - clothes, earrings, little thoughtful knick-knacks - the price was never a concern when it came to buying his dear wife Nannie what she asked for. The reality, as Nannie was used to discovering, was always bound to rear its ugly head. Within mere months of their union taking place, reality struck, and the marriage was crumbling rapidly.

Despite his free and easy use of money, Richard was broke and deep in debt to just about everyone in the town. When he did buy his wife an expensive treat - on some sort of credit - he also purchased a second one for the other girl he had tucked away in town.

Richard's trips to town in his Chevy to visit the stores often struck a suspicious Nannie as taking too long. They couldn't just be casual jaunts, not for the length of time they took him

The more he went to town, the longer his visit was each time. Should Nannie question her husband as to why he spent hours running simple errands, he would play dumb: "Aw, I just dawdled," he would shrug. Still, his wife wasn't one to roll over and accept this lazy explanation. She did a little digging and found out that he was seeing a woman he knew before he proposed to Nannie. Worse still, Richard had no intention of letting go of his mistress.

Nannie had that sinking feeling yet again - she'd made a mistake marrying this man. Still, he'd also made a mistake by marrying a cold-blooded killer.

That winter, a mere couple of months after tying the knot, yet again Nannie answered ads from men in the lonely hearts column in the Kansas paper. She'd make sure she got to the mailbox before everyone else every day. If a letter from a potential suitor was waiting for her, she'd take it to the bathroom to read in peace, swooning as she was swept away into the promise of a better life. The men writing her were led to believe she was widowed, each of them offering to ease her of her loneliness. There was just one thing stopping her from moving on to pastures new. Nannie's fourth husband didn't know it, but his days were numbered.

However, it seems he was spared - for a short while at least - when Nannie's dad died, and her mother announced she was on her way to stay with the couple. With mother there 24/7, Nannie's murderous ideas had to be delayed, although the wicked woman thought of a way around this. She killed her mother.

Perhaps her mother's money was partly a reason for the heartless murder, or maybe her mother found out about Nannie's other men, or maybe she just felt a sudden urge to off her loving parent. Regardless, Nannie would passionately deny poisoning mother Lou, but, considering the symptoms of her death, it's incredibly likely that the older woman did not die of natural causes. After a mere couple of days living with her daughter and son-in-law, she suddenly began suffering chronic stomach pains before passing away.

It seems that Nannie had grown totally devoid of any type of empathy or conscience by this point. Three months later, Richard Morton was buried after suffering the exact same pre-death symptoms as his mother-in-law. As difficult as it is to believe, neither friends nor family asked any questions, and doctors weren't picking up on this repeated pattern of death following Nannie wherever she went. As usual, the black widow wouldn't be on her own for long.

## The Fifth - And Final - Husband

Sam Doss was a clean living, God-fearing man. A sip of alcohol never passed his lips. He'd never smoked, refused to gamble and never, ever said a single cuss word. He certainly didn't run about after women. He was incredibly particular about his appearance and what he wore, beyond thrifty with his money, and lived a simple existence.

To Nannie, he was undeniably boring.

Nearing 60 and taking care of his health, Sam's clean living was plain to see. He looked much younger than his 59 years and had a healthy glow. His tidy dress and conservative hairstyle emanated a wealthy appearance, giving people the sense he was a man who could be trusted. Perhaps it was these things that drew Nannie towards him when he got down on one knee in the summer of 1953.

Sam knew Nannie was a widow. He didn't care to know more than that - he was simply happy to have this woman in his life. He wanted a woman who would stay right by his side 'til death did them part. He would get his wish, partly.

Sam was one of Nannie's many pen-pals. After husband number four was out of the picture, she hopped on the first bus to meet her new suitor. Sam offered Nannie a stark change from her past lovers; he was a state highway inspector who provided steady income, he spoke to her softly and listened to what she had to say, and he took pride in his appearance. He tidied up after himself, helped with the cooking and didn't beat her. To him, she was equal.

Still, this didn't pacify Nannie. Sam was incredibly set in his conservative ways, which annoyed his new wife. He thought her constant reading of romance novels was evil. He saw her use of television as taboo, particularly the love stories she was so enamoured with. Bedtime was always at 9:30 p.m., sex was scheduled, and Nannie was expected to adhere to his routine.

Spending was regulated: The electric fan wasn't to be used until temperatures became beyond unbearable, lights were rarely used even when reading, and furniture was preserved with doilies to prevent having to buy more. Nannie couldn't bear it, so she moved to Alabama. This was more than likely a way to teach her husband a lesson, and if so, it worked. He followed her, pleading to change and for her to come home. He opened up his bank account for her to use freely, giving her equal access. He also took out multiple life insurance policies in his name, citing her as beneficiary. As soon as he did this, he began living on borrowed time.

That September, Sam was at the dinner table ready to polish off Nannie's famous prune cake. Later that evening, he felt a violent pain in his stomach and was retching uncontrollably. He was bedbound, unable to keep anything down and lost 16 pounds. He was sent to the hospital, where he stayed for three weeks.

He was diagnosed with a severe infection of the digestive tract but made an improvement while in hospital and was released at the beginning of October. Nannie, displeased that Sam hadn't succumbed to her poisoning, started where she had left off. She cooked him a hot meal and made him a cup of coffee afterwards, promising that her home cooking would get him back on his feet. Perhaps it would have, but the coffee was laced with arsenic. Before the day was over, Sam Doss had died.

Dr Schwelbein, who had examined Sam before his release from the hospital, was disconcerted to discover that his recovering patient had died. It made no sense - he was getting better.

He quickly ordered an autopsy. As the doctor suspected, Sam's death was not natural. His stomach hosted enough arsenic to kill multiple men.

Police headed straight to Nannie for an explanation, to which she was unable to offer one up. She was subsequently arrested. 'I don't know what you're talking about," the wicked woman would repeat, refusing any suggestions that she poisoned her husband. She would never hurt him, she explained. Even when the police reminded her that arsenic doesn't just add itself to the homemade meal and coffee it was mixed with; she still denied killing Sam. Hours passed as the police tried to get Nannie to pay attention to their questions while she was flicking her way through a romance magazine. Multiple times she was asked to put the magazine down and answer the questions. They were met with giggles. What would normally be seen as an innocent giggle was made sinister when police were sure she was the murderer, and any question was answered with a chuckle.

Getting tired of her laughing instead of talking, Special Agent Ray Page stepped in. Sitting beside the woman, he lit up a cigarette and looked at her. He was sick of her game, of her not offering anything up, of her giggle. He told Nannie as much, noting that, unlike himself and the whole interrogation team, she didn't seem sick or tired at all. Quite the contrary, in fact. Still, nothing from the stoic woman. Eventually, Agent Page laid it all out for Nannie, telling her that they knew about all of her other husbands dying in the exact same way. They'd spoken to other police forces, doctors and pieced things together. Arsenic was Nannie's weapon of choice, but her killing days were over;

all she needed to do was admit it to make it easier for her and everyone involved. Her reaction? To deny all allegations and flick the page on her romance magazine.

Frustration hit new heights. Was Nannie insane, a good actress or just a cold-hearted killer? To find out, he needed to get serious. He pulled the distraction from Nannie's hands, casting the romance magazine aside and demanding answers. The incessant giggling soon stopped. Ray Page was intent on getting the black widow to admit her crimes, and the only thing he could think of now was to appeal to her human side. He pleaded with her to put her demons to rest, to get these crimes off her chest. Their eyes met, and the pair of them knew that the truth was obvious, and Nannie caved; "Alright," Nannie said after a big sigh, "he was a miser." She recounted how Sam Doss wouldn't let her watch TV, how he forced her to sleep without a fan and how he withheld money from her. In Nannie's own words, what's a woman supposed to do under such conditions

It took a little while for officers to work out if the grandmother was serious. They let her talk, confess to the murder of Sam Doss. When she was done, she asked for the romance magazine back. They would comply with her request - but first, they needed to know about the other husbands. Nannie then struck a deal - if she told the police about her late husbands, they would give her the romance magazine back.

And so the tragic stories of Richard Morton, Arlie Lanning and Frank Harrelson were explained in great detail to investigators. All these men were once the apple of Nannie's eye, she would say, but each and every one of them turned out to be nothing but duds. All she ever longed for was true romance, a real man to love her unequivocally, but "dullards" was what she received every time. Should their ghosts be watching over her, Nannie said they'd all be "either drunk or sleeping."

With police getting all of the shocking details from the murderer, they kept up their end of the bargain and handed her the magazine back. Looking at her, it seemed incomprehensible that she was capable of murder. But the evidence suggested otherwise, as did the words coming out of her mouth. Officers asked her what else they had to tell them. After all, it wasn't just husbands who seemed to drop dead around her. Children, grandchildren, her sister and her own mother all died when left with her. Still, Nannie zipped up after confessing to all her ex-husband's murders.

The following morning, detectives from Tulsa, along with Detective Page headed out to North Carolina, Alabama, and Kansas to oversee the exhumations of Nannie's husbands, her mother, her sister, her nephew, and her former mother-in-law. It came to no one's surprise that heavy traces of arsenic were found in every single one of the spouses as well as her own mother. The bodies of the other exhumed possible victims didn't show any arsenic traces but did confirm they'd died by asphyxia, with police believing they'd been smothered in their sleep.

Dubbed as the "husband who got away", Charley Braggs recalled his time as Nannie's first husband as rather unhappy, explaining that she was a serial adulterer. "She was about town more than me," he said while mentioning how he was glad when she finally left for good. He admitted he also grew suspicious of her cooking and, towards the end, was afraid to eat the meals put in front of him.

The state of Oklahoma centred its case on the murder of Sam Doss only, as he died in Tulsa. The other states, where Nannie's trail of victims was coming to light, still needed to try her for the killings that occurred within their jurisdiction. However, she was never tried outside of Oklahoma. She was never convicted of murder other than the killing of Sam Doss because of this.

When reporters had the opportunity to ask Nannie questions when she was being escorted by police, they asked what she thought her repercussions should be for poisoning her husbands. She said, "Why, anything - anything they care to do is all right by me." After many psychiatrists agreed she was mentally sane, Nannie's trial date was given the go-ahead for June 2, 1955, in the Criminal Court of Tulsa. Mere weeks before the trial was due to kick-off, she decided to drop the pantomime and pleaded guilty.

After a short hearing, Judge Adams sentenced Nannie to a life behind bars, not offering up the electric chair as an option because of her gender.

Nannie would look back at her childhood as the root of her adult problems in her later life. A head injury she received when she was around seven seemed to be why she thought she grew up to be a killer. Her family had taken her to visit a relative in Alabama, something that started off as a magical journey seeing as she'd never been off the farm before that. However, the train had to make a sudden stop, which flung Nannie forward where her head collided with the iron seat in front of her. This caused the little girl to suffer blackouts and endure headaches for the rest of her life. There is some correlation between head trauma and becoming a killer, but not enough to excuse the heinous acts Nannie carried out.

The giggling granny died of leukaemia in prison in 1965. She was 59.

# Stephanie Lazarus

This story has fascinated me since I watched a video called *The Interrogation of Stephanie Lazarus* online a couple of years ago. I hadn't known of her crime until then, and her case has been covered rather lightly in comparison to other female killers. Still, this taped interview with her really fascinated me, and after reading this, I suggest you search the title of the video and give it a watch - it exposes someone highly manipulative, dangerous and calculating and catches it all on camera. But first, learn about this truly intriguing case that proves bad deeds tend to find a way to catch up with you.

In 1986, 29-year-old Sherri Rae Rasmussen was just beginning life as a married woman. She was living in a condo with John Ruetten, her husband of three months, and looking forward to all the things life had in store for her: kids, holidays, growing old with John and enjoying the spoils of a charmed life. Those hopes were pulled from beneath her and her new husband in a few short minutes, though, when she was brutally murdered. Why she was killed and who killed would be mysteries that would go unsolved for over two decades.

On the evening of February 24, John Ruetten returned home to a most horrific sight: his wife covered in blood, clearly beaten and violently pumped with bullets, resulting in numerous gunshot wounds covering her chest. Sherri Rae had only been at home because she'd taken the day off work to recover from a back injury she sustained while doing aerobics. With no enemies and no real leads as to who could have done something so callous, police were stuck, and the case didn't advance much at all. However, what was advancing was technology, and this would be the key factor in later helping police crack this case and catch the culprit. Perhaps, though, they weren't prepared to confront what the evidence was telling them; that the murder was committed by one of their own officers.

## A Rising Officer in LA's Police Department

Stephanie Lazarus had been a patrol officer for two years at the time of Sherri Rae's untimely murder. As her career developed, Stephanie became involved with the Drug Abuse Resistance Education program - marketed as DARE to teens in the form of sloganed t-shirts that are still worn today - and visited her former junior high to spread the word about the program. She worked to raise funds to provide round-the-clock childcare for working parents on the force. She also served as a treasurer for the LA Women Police Officers Association for a number of years. She branched out and started her own private investigation business at one point, too, named Unique Investigations.

After an impressive career of over 20 years at LAPD, she was promoted to the high-stakes Art Theft Detail, which served to track stolen art and stomp out art forgeries. She was even featured in the 2009 annual issue of LA People, telling the publication that working the art detail had inspired her to take oil painting classes.

But going back to 1986, Stephanie was still working the streets trying to make it up the ranks. Around this time, she had just come out of a relationship with John Ruetten, and it appeared the split wasn't amicable. While Stephanie was reeling over the demise of this long-term relationship, John was grieving the loss of his new wife.

Investigators had been almost certain the crime had been a robbery gone wrong. Sherri Rae's silver BMW was taken after she'd been murdered, only to turn up ten days later just two miles from her home. Strangely, stereo equipment had been stacked up next to Stephanie's lifeless body, causing police to be almost certain that her killing was the result of a botched robbery.

The police suspicions about the robbery gone awry would be reinforced by a spate of other crimes that occurred just after Sherri Rae's murder. A few days after her brutal killing, two men robbed a woman at gunpoint. A few months later, the criminals held another woman at gunpoint after she walked into them breaking in. Her home was close to Sherri Rae's house. The robbers were described by witnesses as Latino men who were around 5 feet, 4. They became the primary suspects in Sherri Rae's murder, but police never managed to catch them.

As well as the BMW, the only other object stolen from the murder scene ought to have given the investigator's cause for alarm: the newlywed's marriage license had been taken. Another factor weakening the random burglary theory was the deep bite marks left by the murderer on Sherri Rae's arm. A random attacker wouldn't feel the urge to violate the dead woman's body in such an aggressive and personal way.

Months passed with no movement on the case, so the victim's parents began holding press conferences pleading with people who may know something to come forward, offering a $10,000 reward for anyone who could offer up clues. During the investigation, Stephanie Lazarus was merely a tiny blip on the police radar, if that. Numerous pleas from Sherri Rae's father called for the LAPD to consider the facts more closely: his daughter and Stephanie had both dated John Ruetten, and that Stephanie had even turned up at the hospital, where Sherri Rae worked as a nurse, and allegedly threatened her: "If I can't have John," Stephanie spat at her love rival, "then nobody else will."

The bereft parent also recalled another confrontation that occurred a month before the brutal murder. When his daughter had arrived home from work one evening, she was shocked to find Stephanie waiting for her inside, wearing her police uniform. Mere days before the killing, the jilted ex had allegedly called her rival and threatened her, causing a startled Sherri Rae to tell her father that she thought the obsessed officer had been stalking her. At the time, these allegations were dismissed.

The grieving father unbelievably was told to stop watching so much TV. He penned desperate letters to the head of the police department to take a second look at the cold case, but these went unheeded. Eventually, Sherri Rae's father had no choice but to give up.

**Stephanie Lazarus' Evil Deeds Catch Up With Her**

It's ironic that Nels Rasmussen's reports to police had been dismissed as a desperate father making things up after watching too much crime on TV; the way this case eventually unravelled is just like an episode of *Law and Order*.

By February 2009, the Cold Case department of LAPD had some time on their hands due to the declining number of murders occurring in the area, and so they reopened some old cases to see if they could crack them. Investigators proceeded to run DNA tests on old evidence, hoping that newfound technology could help them close some old crimes and perhaps catch a few criminals who thought they'd gotten away with it. Included in this bulk evidence check was the DNA taken from the bite marks on Sherri Rae's body. The test revealed that the murder suspect had to be a female, instantly severing the link to the other robberies in the area. During the initial investigation, Stephanie Lazarus had been interviewed but was never thought of - and as such, never pursued - as a likely suspect. She was, after all, a police officer, and by the time this new evidence bore some fruit, she was high up in the LAPD ranks. Surely, the prime suspect wasn't a police officer?

The officers working this case were faced with a rather uncomfortable situation. A colleague who worked next door - literally, since Stephanie Lazarus' department sat opposite the Cold Case offices - was now a prime suspect in a horrific murder. The team spent a day following the suspect around, eventually managing to take an item discarded by Stephanie that had her saliva on it. It was a match. Over two decades had passed, and nabbing the killer was as easy as that, thanks to DNA testing. On

June 5, 2009, police announced the arrest of Stephanie Lazarus in the cold case, sending shock waves through the press, the public and the LAPD.

Prior to her arrest, she had been sitting in her office when a colleague told her that a suspect currently in custody might have some new information on one of her cases. She left to speak to the "suspect". In accordance with the policy in the building, to get through jail security and meet with a person in custody, she had to hand over her weapon, which she did. She'd walked right into the trap. Unarmed in the jail, 49-year-old Stephanie Lazarus was arrested. Those who worked with her were beyond shocked that the bubbly and vivacious co-worker was capable of such a heinous crime. Her murderous streak was hard to believe for those that spent time in her office, recounting how she was full of hugs and jokes for everyone.

She was described as sweet by neighbours, giving them home-made soaps and chocolate-covered cherries for Christmas. Still, her "sweet" nature wasn't completely concealed. More details about the killer cop began to appear on the Internet. She was known for her erratic behaviour when she was angry or flustered. So much so, some colleague had given her offensive nicknames to mock this.

**Redemption Had Finally Arrived For Sherri Rae's Family**

Sherri Rae's father, Nels Rasmussen, held a press conference to tell the world what he'd been trying to tell the LAPD all along: the most likely suspect is one of your own. He recounted his multiple attempts to get the police to take a closer look at the jealous Stephanie Lazarus' behaviour towards her ex's new spouse.

After the disgraced former police officers arrest, new details emerged. One main part of the puzzle was still missing: the gun that was used to fatally shoot Sherri Rae three times. The LA Times reported that Stephanie had called the police a few weeks after the murder reporting that her car had been broken into on the Santa Monica Pier. She noted all of the things that were stolen: her gym bag, some money, a few clothes, and her 38-caliber handgun. Police, at the time, didn't put two-and-two together.

Looking back at that police report from decades ago, it seems probable that the break-in was a cover-up and police suspect that Stephanie threw her gun in the Pacific Ocean to dispose of the murder weapon.

The murder scene was also more barbaric than had previously been revealed. Sherri Rac had been bludgeoned over the head mercilessly; she had marks on her wrists that suggested she'd been bound by rope or something similar. A robe was strewn on the floor next to the body with bullet holes in it, making it apparent the killer had used it to muffle the gunshots. Frustratingly, the murder may have been avoided had the maid in a nearby apartment called the police when she heard screaming coming from Sherri Rae's house. Sadly, she didn't.

**The Other Side of the Law**

Stephanie Lazarus was now on the wrong side of the law. On June 9, 2009, she appeared in court donning an orange jump suit, acting bewildered and distressed with wide eyes.

Almost three years later, in March 2012, she was found guilty of first-degree murder. During his testimony, John Ruetten said, "The fact that Sherri's death occurred because she met and married me brings me to my knees." A couple of months later on May 11, Stephanie Lazarus was sentenced to 27 years to life in prison, gaining credit for time already served. She will become eligible for parole in 22 years.

Remember to check out the video *The Interrogation of Stephanie Lazarus* to delve a little deeper into this case. It's truly fascinating to watch a cop try and worm her way out of something when she must have known the jig was up.

# Dorothea Puente

Dorothea Helen Puente ran a (now infamous) boarding house in Sacramento, California - but this wasn't just any boarding house. It was a house of cold-blooded murder, fuelled by greed and a complete lack of respect for human life. Those who were killed in the murder house were buried in the backyard of the property.

Born on January 9, 1929, in California, Dorothea's parents worked hard as cotton pickers to take care of their daughter. However, Jesse James and Trudy wouldn't have long to spend with their young child, as both of them died before she was 10. Little Dorothea was sent to an orphanage until relatives from Fresno eventually took her in and took care of her. As she grew older, Dorothea, for whatever reason, lied about her childhood, insisting she was one of three children who were all born and raised in Mexico. Perhaps she was ashamed of being in an orphanage, perhaps she wanted to sound more worldly than she was or perhaps she just wanted to escape the truth of her upbringing, but one thing is clear: lying came naturally to Dorothea.

As 1945 rolled around, Dorothea was blossoming into a young woman, and she married for the first time to a soldier called Fred McFaul. As well as a young bride, she'd also become a young mother, giving birth at 17 and 19. However, Dorothea had no intention of raising these children. The first daughter was sent to live with relatives, and the second little girl was put up for adoption.

Despite not wanting children, Dorothea became pregnant yet again in the late 1940s, but this time she'd not carry the child to full term after suffering a miscarriage. After this, McFaul abandoned the relationship. This utterly humiliated Dorothea, and just like she did about her upbringing, she lied about her failed marriage and claimed that her husband had died of a heart attack.

To support herself, Dorothea forged checks, but law enforcement eventually caught up with her, and she was subsequently sentenced to a year in jail, only to be paroled after serving half her sentence. Not long after her release from jail, Dorothea became pregnant yet again, this time by someone she'd just met. She had another daughter who was yet again put up for adoption. Never single for too long, she married again in 1952 to a Swedish man called Axel Johansson. Their union would last 14 years, but it wouldn't be a smooth-sailing partnership. Still, Dorothea named Axel as her favourite of all her husbands in a 2009 magazine interview - but her long-standing affection towards him was no longer reciprocated by the late 60s, and the pair divorced.

Throughout this marriage, Dorothea was arrested for owning a brothel and was sentenced to three months in Sacramento County Jail. After being released, she was in trouble yet again, getting herself arrested for vagrancy, which saw her sentenced to another stint in jail. Her penchant for breaking the law would only become more serious after this. She got herself a steady job as a nurse's aide, which saw Dorothea caring for elderly and disabled people in their own homes. Pretty quickly after this, she began to manage boarding houses.

After the Johanssen divorce in 1966, she married Roberto Puente, a young man almost half her age. This marriage would only last two years, but it gave her the Spanish surname that's instantly recognisable to any true crime buff - Puente. After yet another failed marriage, Dorothea ended up taking over a three-story care home at 2100 F Street in Sacramento.

During this time, Puente got married again in the mid-70s to Pedro Montalvo, a violent man who was also an alcoholic. The union lasted a mere few months, which was short even by Dorothea's standards. Still, Puente wasn't one to be left on the shelf. She immediately started to scout the local bars, specifically looking for older men who were in receipt of benefits. She reverted back to her old ways by forging their signatures to steal their money, but she was caught yet again. Not deterred by law enforcement, while still on probation for the fraud crimes, she continued to commit the very same fraud on unsuspecting older men. In 1981, Dorothea began renting one of the upstairs apartments at 1426 F Street in Sacramento.

## The Twisted Crimes Escalate from Petty to Murderous

Some of the other tenants in the building liked Dorothea, particularly since she would cook them meals. Others weren't so fond of her; they found her tight-fisted and difficult (such as withholding their mail from them). Perhaps those tenants who disliked Dorothea were wary of her because they sensed something quietly malevolent from the woman. Still, likely nothing could convince them that the middle-aged woman posed a real danger to them and all of the other tenants who resided in the building.

Puente saw people as meal tickets, purely there to fund her lifestyle. It's been estimated by police that her nefarious actions were bringing her more than $5,000 in cash a month - more than enough to live on comfortably, especially in the early 80s.

Fraud and fleecing unsuspecting men eventually weren't enough for Dorothea.

The murders began not long after she began renting out a room at 1426 F Street. In April of '82, Ruth Monroe, Dorothea's 61-year-old supposed friend, moved in with Puente in her top floor apartment but quickly became ill. Despite being fit and healthy before residing with her friend, Ruth soon found herself bedbound. Nobody knew what was up with the sick woman, but at least she had her good pal Dorothea there to take care of her - or so people thought. It wasn't long before Ruth died in an apparent suicide. She'd consumed fatal amounts of codeine and Tylenol. Dorothea told the police that her friend was suffering from a deep bout of depression since her husband was terminally ill. Authorities believed her version of events, and the death was ruled a suicide.

A couple of weeks later, the police were back at 1426 F Street when pensioner Malcolm McKenzie accused Dorothea of drugging him and stealing from him. For this, she was convicted of three charges of theft and was sentenced to five years in jail on August 18, 1982. Still, there was no containing her need to acquire elderly men to take advantage of - even in jail, she was plotting how she would sustain her lifestyle when she was released. She started writing to a 77-year-old retiree Everson Gillmouth from Oregon. Their pen-pal friendship developed into a romantic relationship, and when Dorothea was eventually released in 1985 (only serving three years of the five-year term), Everson was waiting to pick her up in his red Ford truck. Their relationship escalated quickly, and wedding plans were made briskly. They moved into the unassuming death trap that was the upstairs apartment at 1426 F Street.

In November that year, Dorothea hired Ismael Florez, a local handyman, to install some wood panelling through her apartment. The pair had a strange arrangement, however; for Ismael's labour plus $800, Dorothea handed him the keys to a red Ford truck, which according to her, belonged to her boyfriend in LA, who wanted rid of it. She also asked the work-hungry handyman to build her a box that was precisely 6 feet by 3 feet by 2 feet, which she told him was for "storage." Once he built this for her, Ismael's work wasn't yet over - he was asked to transport it to a storage depot once Dorothea had filled it and nailed it tightly shut. The older woman insisted on accompanying Ismael as he took the heavy wooden box to the storage place, but on the way, she changed her mind. She decided she wanted to dump the "junk" on a riverbank that also served as a makeshift dumping site.

The following January in 1986, a man who was fishing on the river spotted the large, ominous-looking box sitting just feet from the river bank and called the police. Investigators arrived and prized open the crudely made casket, discovering a badly decomposing body of an elderly man callously stuffed inside. The body was so decomposed that police weren't able to identify the victim.

Meanwhile, Dorothea continued to collect Everson Gill mouth's pension checks and even penned letters to his family telling them that he was ill, hence the reason he'd not been in touch. In reality, he'd been snuffed out by the older woman and dumped by the river to rot.

At the same time, her room and board business was booming and Dorothea took on 40 new tenants. Despite Everson's body being found, it remained unidentified for three years and allowed Dorothea to keep drawing his pension fraudulently.

She continued to accept elderly tenants, possibly purely to use them for their pension money. The murderous landlord was also popular with the local social workers because of her willingness to take in those who were deemed to be difficult individuals, such as drug addicts and abusive tenants. Dorothea collected the tenants' mail before they had a chance to and gave them a monthly allowance, pocketing the remainder for herself for "expenses."

During this time, parole agents visited Dorothea, who was breaching the order she'd been given to stay clear of the elderly and avoid handling any government checks. These agents visited 1426 F Street no less than fifteen times, and none of these violations was ever noted.

However, she couldn't evade suspicion forever. Questions were first raised when neighbours picked up on the odd day-to-day activities of a homeless alcoholic known around the area as "Chief." Dorothea said she's "adopted" the man, and he was her handyman, which also sounded slightly off. Chief, or

Dorthoea's request, dug up the basement and carted the soil and rubble away in a wheelbarrow. Chief also later took down a garage situated in the backyard and placed fresh concrete down. Soon after this, Chief vanished for good.

In November 1988, police attended 1426 F Street yet again after the sudden disappearance of tenant Alvaro Montoya, a schizophrenic man whose worried social worker had reported him missing. Upon arriving at the property, police noticed the disturbed soil and decided to take a closer look by digging it up. They uncovered the body of 78-year-old tenant Leona Carpenter. This prompted them to do a more thorough dig of the area, which unearthed seven more bodies.

## The Killer Was Hiding in Plain Sight

Dorothea wasn't a suspect - and why would she be? She was a frail old lady. Of course, she was on the police's radar, but that was for crimes of fraud, not cold-blooded murder. There was no way she could have done this, or so the police thought. While the property was being turned upside down, Dorothea was allowed to leave to buy a coffee, which she did before taking off and fleeing to LA. Here she was up to her old tricks again, befriending a pensioner she met in a bar. The elderly man, however, recognised Dorothea from the numerous reports about the murder house on TV and swiftly called the authorities. She was arrested, and finally, the 'Death House Landlady' as the press had dubbed her, was no longer free to slay innocent lodgers.

Her trial took place in Monterey County, California, in October 1992 and stretched over a year. Prosecutor John O'Mara called over a staggering 130 witnesses. His argument to the jury was that Dorothea spiked her tenants with sleeping pills and suffocated them. She then paid convicts to dig holes in the yard, which would serve as a graveyard of sorts.

The defence also called several witnesses that painted Dorothea as a generous and caring woman, one of whom was her long-lost daughter. They all testified how the kind older woman had helped them and even been a factor in them having successful careers. Experts on mental health also testified of Dorothea's troubled and abusive upbringing and offered their take on how it motivated her in her bid to help those in need. Still, they couldn't disagree with the fact that she had a malignant side brought on by the stress and pressures of caring for her often difficult tenants.

O'Mara rebuffed this by asking the jury to consider that her victims were human beings who had nothing in this world except their social security checks or pensions, which callous Dorothea took full advantage of before and after killing them. He suggested that sentencing her to death was the only punishment.

After a number of days of jury deliberations, they were deadlocked at 7–5 for life. The judge then declared a mistrial when the jury decided that further deliberations wouldn't change their minds on sentencing. Under the law, this meant Dorothea received life behind bars without the possibility of parole. She was locked up at Central California Women's Facility. She never admitted to the murders and always maintained her innocence, stating until the very end that all her tenants had passed away of "natural causes."

Dorothea passed away on March 27, 2011, behind bars at the age of 82.

# Aileen Wuornos

Possibly the most infamous person in this book, Aileen Wuornos has become something of the poster child for all female killers. Painted to be a man-hating, psychotic killer who lusted for blood, Aileen was framed as crazy by everyone. Her family, the police, and almost everyone she'd known in her life had nothing but disdain for her.

Was she violent and aggressive with a warped sense of right and wrong? Absolutely. She snuffed out men's lives without a second thought, unrepentant enough to not only steal from their lifeless bodies but also brazen enough to drive around in their cars after their deaths. She hated human life and said so much herself, but this kind of hatred doesn't spawn out of nowhere. Her life, from beginning to end, was full of abuse, exploitation and depravity. Aileen was born into a life of torture, eventually becoming the torturer.

There's an abundance of written words available about Aileen Wuornos. Some of that is true: she killed seven men as she made her way around Florida. She was a sex worker, and this was how she found her victims. She confessed to these murders to avoid her lover, Tyria Moore, being implicated in the crimes. Aileen's most infamous moments, or at least the moments most people associate with her, are caught on camera; her profane outburst in the courtroom telling the Judge that she hopes his wife and kids get raped is etched into people's memories.

There is, however, an abundance of myths peddled as fact about Aileen and her crimes. One of them being that she wa America's first female serial killer. Although that sentence doe help sell more books and offer more sensational headlines, it' simply not true. Aileen's crime spree occurred in the '80s - con sidering that women have been spree killing and murdering se rially as long as men have been, this is an extreme bending o the truth that has been widely accepted as fact.

Aileen's activities as a sex worker have often been heavily fo cused upon in news articles and TV shows covering her crim spree. However, these too are erroneously exaggerated, al though some of these 'facts' came directly from Aileen herself she claims to have had sex with 250,000 clients (*Berry-Dee Monster, 2006*). This was then reported as fact, despite such feat requiring her to sleep with three dozen men each day, ever day, over the span of almost 20 years. It would certainly be tough world record to beat if it were true. Still, this doesn't sto the press from touting this near-impossible feat as somethin Aileen accomplished.

Despite the senseless lying, the pure evil in her actions and he sheer disdain for human life, she remains intriguing. She is de plorable, wicked, pitiful, wronged, and abused all at once. Per haps no other killer can evoke such feelings of simultaneous re vulsion and sympathy. To top off her story, she was befriende and later adopted by Arlene Pralle, who Aileen later turned on Add on her life backstory screaming "never had a chance", an you have a tale that reads like a movie.

**An Abusive Upbringing**

Aileen's father, Leo Pittman, was a convicted paedophile and a cruel sociopath who hanged himself in prison in the late sixties. Diane Wuornos was only fifteen when she married Leo, and she gave birth to two of his children. She divorced him a couple of years into their marriage, just before Aileen was brought into the world. However, Diane struggled with bringing up two small children at such a young age, and in 1960, she left Aileen and her older brother, Keith, with her mother and father. Lauri and Britta would bring up the abandoned children alongside their own brood.

The pair raised their grandchildren in Troy, Michigan. However, they didn't reveal that they were the youngsters' grandparents, bringing them up as their own children. Aileen eventually found out the truth when she was twelve, compounding to a traumatic childhood whereby she'd already been the subject of abuse by other children, including her brother. Lauri was a heavy drinker and didn't think twice about taking the belt to the children when he felt they misbehaved.

Aileen was also allegedly passed around the local boys as a youngster, trading her body for cigarettes or money. Sometimes, for nothing. A lot of the boys in the area lost their virginity to Aileen, perhaps more than would admit it. Her brother Keith would also have his way with his sister from the age of 10 when he started pursuing incestuous encounters with his younger sibling.

However, when Aileen and her brother found out their parentage, they rebelled against his strictness and became unruly. By age fourteen, Aileen was pregnant. She was subsequently sent to an unwed mothers' home.

Here, she was hostile and seemed incapable of getting on with her peers. Her baby, a little boy, was put up for adoption in early 1971. Fast forward six months to July of '71, Britta Wuornos passed away. Aileen's safety net - what little one she had - was surely being snatched away. Her mother, Diane, offered to let her and her brother come live with her, but they turned down her offer. They didn't want to travel to Texas and be bound by her strict rules for the household. Lee, as Wuornos started to go by, subsequently dropped out of school to hitchhike and earn money as a sex worker.

In the years that followed, Lauri killed himself, and Keith died of throat cancer. In the wake of these deaths, Lee made her way to Florida, meeting an elderly man called Lewis Fell. He had an abundance of money from investing in stocks, which set off dollar signs in Aileen's eyes. Lee and Lewis were quickly married - but not for long.

The short-lived marriage ended when Lewis was granted a restraining order and an annulment after his new bride hurled a cue ball at a bartender's head while out on a drinking binge. He said Lee had frittered away all of his money and even beat him with his walking stick when he refused to front her more cash. It seems Lee wasn't bad at getting money at this point in her life - it was keeping it that appeared to be the issue.

There was also the money she received from Keith's life insurance. Lee got $10,000, which she squandered in two months. This is upwards of $30,000 when adjusted for inflation. It would be hard to spend $500 a day now, let alone in the '80s, but Aileen still found a way to do this and still have nothing to show for it. She drifted around Florida for the next decade, tricking, hitchhiking, and drinking. She funded her beer habit with theft and forgery, even doing a small stint in jail for an armed robbery.

From failed relationship to failed relationship, Lee wasn't exactly lucky in love. In fact, it's doubtful she knew what love was until she met twenty-four-year-old Tyria Moore. Lee got talking to her in a gay bar in 1986, a time when she was lonely, frustrated at life and ready for a change. In the beginning, it was idyllic. Ty seemed to adore her lover, and Lee was enamoured by the fact her girlfriend hadn't up and left her as everyone else did. Ty quit her maid job while Lee supported her by doing stints of sex work. The passion would fizzle somewhat when the money ran dry, though, but Ty still stuck with Lee, the pair hopping from motel to motel.

Lee, contrary to popular belief, was never hugely successful in pulling tricks. Their lifestyle, as meagre as it was, became hard to fund. They - or rather, Lee - had to do something about that.

## A Spate of Peculiar Murders

Richard Mallory was a middle-aged man who owned an electronics repair shop in Clearwater, Florida. He was known for his erratic behaviour - he would often close up his shop without warning and take off for days at a time. He'd spend this time drinking and indulging in sex binges. His lifestyle brought him a lot of paranoia - he was said to have changed his apartment locks almost ten times in three years.

He was an erratic employer, too. He kept employees on long enough to get through the backlog of work that piled up during one of his binges, then let them go. He had three main constants in his life - sex, drink and a perpetual state of paranoia. When he no-showed for work in December 1989, no one really batted an eyelid.

He never let anyone close enough to him to notice that he was gone for much longer than normal. It was only when his Cadillac was discovered around Daytona that anyone suspected something was wrong. In mid-December, two men were searching for scrap metal along a dirt road near Interstate 95 in Volusia County, Florida. Instead of junk to resell, they stumbled upon a corpse hidden in a discarded roll of carpet.

Fingerprints taken from the decomposing hands confirmed the man was Richard Mallory. Three bullets from a .22 had sealed his fate. Months of investigation exposed Richard's seedy lifestyle and shady contacts but offered up no real clues to his murder. An initial suspect was a stripper he frequented called Chastity, but the little evidence turned up here led to nowhere. The case went from cold to ice cold.

In May of 1990, the body of a naked man was found in Brooks County, Georgia, close to the Florida state line. .22 calibre slugs were found in the man's body. Again, nobody had any dea about the death, and no clues were found. The following month, in June, yet another man was found dead in the picturesque woods of Citrus County, Florida.

He was identified as David Spears, who was last seen in mid-May. His truck was discovered not long after his body, parked up on Interstate 75, unlocked with the plates missing. Thirty miles away in Pasco County, another man was found naked and murdered, just off Interstate 75.

His body was so badly decomposed that medical examiners couldn't ID him nor figure out a rough date of death. He had nine bullets pumped into him, all from a .22 calibre. Pasco County police had no luck identifying this man, but they'd heard about a similar case occurring in Citrus County. Pasco police got in touch with Marvin Padgett from the Citrus County Police Department, and they discussed the similarities in the case. They agreed to stay in touch and be sure to let each other know if they get any leads.

Pasco also got in touch with the Georgia Bureau of Investigation, and the similarities between each dead man were noted, but at the moment, it was nothing but speculation - there wasn't enough evidence here to pull together a strong investigation.

## The Killing Spree Continues While Police Are at a Loss

On a humid July day in 1990, a driver lost control of their car, and it hurtled off the road near Orange Springs, Florida. The smoking vehicle eventually came to a halt in some bushes.

Rhonda Bailey was out on her porch as she watched the car
nage unfold in front of her. She spotted two women emerg
from the busted-up car, frantically tossing beer cans aroun
and yelling profanities at one another. She observed that th
brown-haired woman was the quieter of the two; she was
stark contrast to the taller blonde woman, with the bleedin
arm and bellowing loud mouth.

The blonde woman walked up to Rhonda's porch and begge
her not to call the police, claiming her dad's house was just u
the road. After bargaining with the crash witness, the pair go
back in the damaged car, in spite of its smashed windshield
and drove off. They wouldn't get far, though - the car brok
down a mile or so down the road. The couple abandoned th
car and set off walking, leaving the vehicle smoking by th
roadside. A volunteer at Orange Spring Fire Department re
sponded to a call about the burning car and bumped into th
two women as they walked away from the wreckage. He aske
them if they owned the car and needed help; the mouth
blonde yelled at him, cursing him until he left them alone. Th
couple continued walking.

Police were called, and sheriff's deputies headed to the wreck
age. The grey 1988 Pontiac Sunbird's interior was filled wit
smashed glass from the windshield. Bloodstains adorned th
car seats, and the license plate had been stripped.

A search of the vehicle insurance number showed that the ca
was owned by Peter Siems. Peter had been missing since June
after setting off from Jupiter, Florida, to go stay with relative
in Arkansas. He was 65-years-old and since retiring had spen

a lot of his spare time working with a Christian outreach ministry. It was clear something sinister had happened to Peter, so Jupiter Police sent out a teletype to other police forces with descriptions of the two women seen leaving the car wreckage near Orange Springs. Sketches of the two female suspects were also drawn up and distributed. It was a waiting game now - but with no leads, and the state of Peter's vehicle, police weren't optimistic about finding him alive.

Troy Burress set off for work at Gilchrist Sausage in the early hours of July 30. When he didn't report back to the depot later that day, his manager began calling around and was shocked to find that Tony hadn't turned up for his last few deliveries. Time went by, and Tony's family were beginning to panic - this wasn't like him at all. At 2:00 am the following day, Burress's wife went to the police to report him missing. By 4:00 am, sheriff's deputies from the Marion County department located his abandoned truck by the side of State Road 19. Tony was nowhere in sight.

After four days had passed with no word from Tony, his wife and family were beside themselves. On day five, a picnicking family stumbled upon his dead body in the Ocala National Forest, roughly eight miles from where his truck had been abandoned.

The humidity and intense heat of the Florida sun accelerated the body's decomposition, hindering an accurate identification at the crime scene, but his grief-stricken wife managed to identify his wedding ring. He was killed with two bullets from a .22 calibre, one in the back, one in the chest. The initial prime suspect was a known drifter and hitchhiker called Curtis Blankenship. He'd been seen hitchhiking up Highway 19 the same day Tony disappeared and was picked not far from his abandoned work truck. However, as this line of investigation unravelled, it became obvious Curtis had no involvement in the murder. Yet again, police were stumped.

## Police Were Convinced They Were Hunting a Female Killer

Dick Humphreys was working his last day at the Department of Health and Rehabilitative Services in Florida. He was due to start a new career in Ocala, working with abused children. He never made it home that night. The 56-year-old former police chief had just celebrated his 35th wedding anniversary the day before. On September 11, he was gone.

The following day, he was discovered in Marion County with seven .22 calibre slugs penetrating his lifeless body.

Walter Gino Antonio was found a month later on an old dirt road in Dixie County. The 60-year-old had been shot four times with the elusive .22. When he was found in mid-November, he'd not been dead for long - the police were just behind the killers, never quite catching them.

The commander of the Marion County Sheriff's Criminal Investigation Division, Steve Binegar, knew all about the spate of killings in Citrus and Pasco. The similarities were impossible to ignore. As the crimes unfolded, he was following closely, alongside a multi-agency task force that had representatives from each county where victims were discovered. It was established that hardly anyone would take the risk to pick up hitchhikers anymore, but if someone did, they would have to be certain the person they were picking up wasn't a threat. This led to Steve Binegar suspecting a female killer, possibly even two - specifically, the pair of women who had crashed and abandoned Peter Siems's car and took off.

He looked to the press for help in getting some leads. Reuters ran a story about the murders in late November, publicly stating that police were looking for the women. News outlets across Florida picked up the unusual story and ran it alongside the police sketches of the female suspects.

By mid-December, leads were pouring in. The police obtained numerous tips involving the same two women, one, in particular, offering them their names. Someone in Homosassa Springs rented the pair a trailer a year prior and told police their names were Tyria and Lee. After that, a woman in Tampa said the two women had worked at her motel. She also offered up their names; she said one was called Tyria Moore, and the other one was Susan Blahovec.

Then an anonymous caller identified the suspects as Lee Blahovec and Tyria Moore. Lee was apparently the dominant one, the caller noted, telling the cops that the pair were lovers although Lee was a truck stop prostitute. The police were finally getting somewhere.

The real leads, though, were from Port Orange. Their police force was already tracking women by the names of Lee Blahovec and Tyria Moore due to their suspicious behaviour and could offer up a detailed account of the pair's movements from September through to mid-December.

The duo had stayed at the Fairview Motel in Harbor Oaks, although Blahovec had registered herself as Cammie Marsh Greene, another of her aliases.

They also rented a tiny apartment close to the Fairview, but money issues saw them return to the motel. They eventually left in early December, although Blahovec/Greene stayed there on her own until December 10. A computer check came up with the driver's license and criminal record of Tyria Moore as well as the aliases Susan Blahovec and Cammie Marsh Greene. Tyria didn't have a serious record by any means, with the one charge of breaking and entering filed against her in 1983 having been dropped. Blahovec had a trespassing arrest on file, and there was nothing on Greene's record. The photo on Blahovec's driver's license didn't match the one on Greene's.

However, it was the picture on Greene's ID that offered up the best leads. Volusia County officers visited pawnshops in the local area and found that in Daytona, Greene had pawned in multiple items including a camera and a radar detector. As certain states require a thumbprint alongside ID when pawning in goods, there was a thumbprint on the receipt of items exchanged for money. The items pawned in belonged to Richard Mallory. The net was closing in, particularly when police went to a pawn shop in Ormond Beach and found Greene had pawned tools that matched the ones taken from David Spears' abandoned vehicle.

The thumbprint was the breakthrough, though. A hand search of fingerprint records at Volusia County showed a match to that of 'Greene'. However, those weapons charges and an outstanding warrant was against Lori Grody. The bloody palm print taken from Peter Siems's car matched Lori Grody's fingerprint too. This abundance of information was immediately sent over to the National Crime Information Center, prompting responses from Michigan, Colorado and Florida, helping police finally connect the dots; Grody, Blahovec and Greene were all aliases for one woman: Aileen Carol Wuornos.

**Now They Have a Name, The Hunt for Aileen Wuornos Begins**

The hunt for the murderer started around January 5, 1991. Officers were paired up with two undercover drug dealers called "Bucket" and "Drums" in the hopes of tracking her down. On January 8, officers Mike Joyner and his partner Dick Martin, disguised as their undercover personas, "Bucket" and "Drums," found Aileen drinking at the Port Orange Pub. However, they didn't plan on her arrest being as straightforward as heading up to her, cuffing her and marching her down to the station. They were seeking an airtight case and intended to get to know her, allow her to trust them a little and go from there.

This plan was almost thwarted when Port Orange police suddenly burst in and took Aileen outside. Mike Joyner, aka "Drums", panicked and phoned the command post located at a nearby motel, which houses authorities from six different jurisdictions who were involved with the case. The Volusia County Sheriff's Office immediately spoke with the Port Orange police force and requested that they don't arrest Aileen, no matter what.

This was relayed to eager-to-arrest cops just in time, and Aileen was freed and headed back to the bar. The undercover police then took the opportunity to strike up a conversation with her buying her time with some beers. She decided to leave the Port Orange Pub bar at 10:00 pm, declining Bucket and Drums' offer of a ride home. The wary takedown of Aileen wasn't quite going to plan. As the inebriated woman walked down Ridgewood Avenue, two officers pulled up behind Aileen, trialling her. As she made it to the next watering hole, the now infamous biker bar, the Last Resort, Bucket and Drums turned up bought her more beers and resumed their conversation.

They departed not long after midnight, but Aileen didn't leave the bar at all that night. Her last night of freedom was spent asleep in the Last Resort.

The next afternoon, Bucket and Drums came back to the bar where Aileen was still drinking. They spent the day talking to her, all the while wearing transmitters that made sure the police were aware of everything that was going on. Their plan was to make their move later that evening, but the Last Resort was setting the place up for a big barbecue, and bikers were due to flock to the bar at any moment readying themselves for an evening of beer, food, and rowdiness.

This prompted the police to go ahead and arrest Aileen. Bucket and Drums offered Aileen the chance to get herself freshened up at their motel room, which she accepted before leaving with them. As she stepped outside, Larry Horzepa from the Marion County Sheriff's Office walked straight up to her, showed his badge and told her she was being arrested due to the outstanding warrant against Lori Grody. There was purposefully no mention of the murders, and police remained tight-lipped towards the media about the breakthrough in arresting the murder suspect. They had good reason for this cautious approach; they didn't have a murder weapon, nor had they managed to find Tyria Moore.

## The Police Obtain a Confession

By January 10, police managed to track down Aileen's partner in crime. She was staying with her sister in Pennsylvania. Jerry Thompson of Citrus County and Bruce Munster from Marion County police headed straight over to interview her. Her rights were read, but she wasn't charged with anything. The officers made sure Tyria knew what perjury meant, swore her in, and let her offer up her statement.

It was revealed she knew about the murders ever since Lee returned home driving Richard Mallory's car. She said Lee had confessed to killing a man that day, but Tyria insisted she wanted to hear no more and asked Lee to keep it to herself. She said this pattern was repeated every time she brought something new home and tried to tell her about where it came from. Ty admitted she had her suspicions as to what was going on but didn't want to know what Lee was really up to. The more she found out, the more she would feel like she had to report her girlfriend to the police. Plus, she said, she was scared of Aileen. "She always said she'd never hurt me, but then you can't believe her, so I don't know what she would have done."

The following day, Tyria headed back to Florida with the officers to assist the ongoing investigation. A confession from Lee would make the case against her practically airtight, which was the end goal. This was all explained to Tyria on the flight back to Florida. They put her up in Daytona with the request that she make contact with Lee in jail. Ty's being back in Florida was covered up with the explanation that she'd been given some money from her mother and used it to come down and collect the rest of her belongings.

The phone conversations were to be recorded, and Tyria was to stress to Aileen that the police had been questioning her family, and she felt she was going to be blamed for the murderers that Lee had committed. Officers hoped that, out of loyalty to her former girlfriend, Aileen would cave in and confess to her crimes.

The first call was on January 14, with Lee still believing that she was behind bars for the Lori Grody violations. When Tyria broached her worries about Lee's murders being pinned on her, she was reassured by her ex. Lee pointed out that she was only in jail for the concealed weapons charge as well as an old traffic ticket. "I read the newspaper, and I wasn't one of those little suspects," Lee told her former lover.

She wasn't stupid, though; she was all too aware that the phones in jail were monitored, and this knowledge was made aware by her use of code words and obviously constructed alibis. "I think somebody, where you worked, said something; that it looked like us," she said, "It's a case of mistaken identity." The police could see through her blatant attempts at deflecting her guilt, and her lack of confession was beginning to frustrate them. They needed her to admit to what she'd done. The rigmarole continued for another three days.

Tyria stepped up her insistence that the police were hunting her for the crimes, and it became obvious that Aileen came to understand what Ty expected of her. Lee even voiced her distrust that Tyria was having the conversations taped. Still, Aileen stopped being as careful about what she said. She began openly expressing that she'd never let Ty go down for crimes she didn't commit. "I'm not going to let you go to jail," Lee promised, "Listen, if I have to confess, I will." On the morning of January 16, that's exactly what she did.

She gave her confession to Larry Horzepa and Bruce Munster, making it abundantly clear that Ty was in no way involved in the murders throughout. She was also vehement that none of her crimes was her fault; they were all carried out in self-defence. Each man she killed had either beaten her, threatened her with violence, or had raped her. Should she blurt out something potentially incriminating, she would go back on her words and retell them to suit her narrative. She'd been raped multiple times over the last couple of years and was pissed, she said. Each of her victims had become aggressive towards her, and out of fear, she murdered them.

A spate of lucrative book and movie offers made their way to the laps of detectives, Lee's relatives, Tyria and even to Aileen herself. She seemed to be under the impression that she'd become a millionaire from her unbelievable story, not knowing that Florida prohibits criminals from profiting from their crimes.

**Born-Again Christian Arlene Pralle Steps in And Adopts Lee**

Arlene Pralle, a born-again Christian in her mid-forties joined the pandemonium after sending Aileen a letter, explaining how Jesus told her to reach out after she saw the story in the newspaper. The letter had enclosed Arlene's home phone number, and by the end of January, Lee made her first collect call to her soon-to-be passionate defender. It didn't take long for Arlene to tell her new friend that everyone was trying to profit from her story. Subsequently, Aileen asked for and received new attorneys.

Arlene was sought after by reporters, whom she told she felt like she was trapped in jail with Lee. She compared herself and Aileen as being Jonathan and David from the bible, explaining how each knew what the other was thinking and feeling. "If the world could know the real Aileen Wuornos, there's not a jury that would convict her," she said. Throughout this time, Arene was regularly on talk shows, and her quotes were plastered over the tabloids. She'd talk to anyone who would listen about Aileen and her case.

She organised interviews for reporters with Aileen, thinking this would buy public sympathy, although it only served to offer Lee a platform to further spin and twist her story. The pair of them focused on Aileen's undeniably troubled upbringing, and they also flung accusations of corruption towards the agents tendering the book and movie deals, as well as the detectives dealing with the case, the attorneys and, most of all, Tyria Moore.

In November of 1991, Arlene Pralle legally adopted Aileen. This was because a message from God had told her to.

## The Trial Begins

Aileen's new attorneys worked out a plea bargain, in which she pleaded to six charges to receive six consecutive life terms. One state attorney disagreed, however, and thought the death penalty was the best way to obtain justice for her crimes. On January 14, 1992, the trial for the murder of Richard Mallory went ahead, and the amount of evidence and number of witnesses against Aileen was irrevocably damaging to her case.

The medical examiner who performed the autopsy on Richard Mallory's body explained how the man had taken between ten and twenty minutes to die, which would have been incredibly agonising and frightening for him. Tyria testified that Lee wasn't upset after the killing, nor was she drunk or nervous when she confessed to her about murdering him. A dozen different men attended court to tell them of their encounters with Aileen while she worked along Florida's highways.

There's a law in Florida called the 'Williams Rule' that permit evidence relating to different crimes to be admitted to th court if it helps to prove a pattern of behaviour. Because of this all the details regarding the other murders were presented t the jury.

Aileen's version of events, where she killed only in self-defence would have been believable if the jury had only been given th Richard Mallory case. The jury was instead made aware of ever other murder, which made the idea of them all being in self-de fence highly improbable. Excerpts from her taped confessio were played to the court, only serving to make her self-defenc claims seem even more far-fetched. The tape of her confessin appeared to show a confident killer, not at all bothered by th tale she was telling. She was heard making idle chit-chat with her interrogators and told her public defender to be quiet nu merous times. Her image up on the screen spoke to the jury, es pecially when she said she deserved to die.

One of Aileen's public defenders, Tricia Jenkins, was agains her client testifying and told her as much. Still, she insiste on getting up and telling her story, but by this point, her vei sion of Richard Mallory's murder bore next to no resemblanc to the version she gave in her confession. She explained ho he'd sodomised and raped her before and after torturing he Cross-examination, however, annihilated her at the stand an ripped whatever credibility she may have had to shreds. Prose cutor John Tanner exposed all of her lies she'd been caught up in and highlighted all of her inconsistencies. When faced with this, she became agitated and was visibly seething. Aileen was the defence's only witness, and by the time she was done, there was no real doubt as to how the trial was going to play out.

On January 27, the jury returned to court with their verdict: guilty of first-degree murder. When they exited the courtroom, Aileen unleashed her rage on them, shouting, "I'm innocent! I was raped! I hope you get raped!" This outburst was going to be at the forefront of jurors minds as the penalty phase was set to begin the following day. They wouldn't forget the woman they'd come to know throughout the trial, nor would they forgive her horrifying words. Unanimously, they recommended that she be sentenced to the electric chair. The Judge agreed.

Aileen never stood trial again. Later that year, in an attempt to "get right" with God, she pleaded no contest to the murders of Dick Humphreys, Troy Burress and David Spears. She still insisted that Richard Mallory raped her, but stated the others didn't - they only attempted to. The monologue ended with her screaming to Assistant State Attorney Ric Ridgeway, "I hope your wife and children get raped." In mid-May, Judge Thomas Sawaya gave her another three death sentences, to which Aileen replied with, "Motherfucker." By June that year, she pleaded guilty to killing Charles Carskaddon, which gave her a fifth death sentence.

For a short while, there were some rumours that Aileen could receive a new trial for the slaughter of Richard Mallory. Uncovered evidence exposed Richard Mallory as a sex offender, something the jury had no knowledge of. He'd served a decade behind bars for sexual violence, and Lee's attorneys felt that the outcome would have been different should this information have been brought forward. No new trial was given, however.

Aileen was executed by lethal injection on the morning of October 9, 2002. She was 46. She'd spent almost a decade on death row for her crimes. The execution took place at Florida State Prison.

Some of her last words were, "I'll be back like Independence Day with Jesus, June 6, like the movie, big mothership and all. I'll be back." I can't help but wonder what Aileen Wuornos' fate would be had she been caught for her crimes in this day and age. She was clearly unhinged, and her behaviour doesn't mimic that of a mentally healthy individual. Should she have been kept locked up? Absolutely. Perhaps somewhere that understood her mental state more than prison did. The things she did were vile and abhorrent, as were the things she endured throughout her life. Maybe someone like Aileen should have been studied, her trauma fully understood and her behaviour leading up to the murders recognised so we can work to prevent such crimes in the future.

# Beverley Allitt

If you often watch crime documentaries (like me), then you'll perhaps be familiar with this case. I've watched numerous episodes of crime shows dedicated to Beverley Allitt, and each time I'm shocked, saddened, angered and confused by her actions. Her deplorable crimes saw her dubbed as the '*Angel of Death*' by the press, and she was front-page news for quite some time in the UK from 1991. Not only is she one of Britain's most notorious female serial killers, but she's also reviled for the helpless victims she chose - young children. What makes this even worse is that she was the person who was supposed to take care of these babies and ensure their safety. She was a nurse entrusted to comfort, help and tend to sick children. The premise itself is terrifying, particularly if you're a parent, but to know that this woman was able to carry out these murderers is even more frightening.

Beverley was one of four children and showed signs of alarming behaviour from a young age. She would wear casts and dressings over small wounds, drawing attention to herself by her perceived bad injuries. She wouldn't allow these wounds or injuries to be checked out, so it could be that they were often imagined.

As she entered her teens, she went from a chubby child to gaining weight rapidly, eventually becoming overweight. Her attention-seeking acts also gained traction, as did her aggressive streak. She spent an unusual amount of time in hospitals getting medical attention for multiple physical ailments, which ended up with her perfectly healthy appendix removed. This would take much longer than normal to heal as Beverley wouldn't stop interfering with the wound after surgery. She frequently self-harmed, too. In the end, she had to change doctors at an alarming rate as they all became wise to her attention-seeking. As soon as one doctor gently made her aware they knew what she was doing, she'd hop over to a new doctor's practice.

As such, there was only one job she would ever pursue as a career: she trained to be a nurse. Still, her odd behaviour continued. Her peers suspected her of smearing faeces on the nursing home walls where she trained. Her spate of illnesses and ailments also saw her have a high absentee level. Her partner at the time later testified that she was deceptive, aggressive, and extremely manipulative, even going as far as lying about being pregnant and being raped.

Regardless of her poor attendance, inability to mix with her nursing peers and failing her nursing examinations, she was given a temporary six-month contract at the Grantham and Kesteven Hospital in Lincolnshire. The place was perpetually understaffed, which is likely why Allitt was able to secure herself a place working on Children's Ward 4. There were only two nurses working the day shift and one for the night, which is probably a big factor in how Beverley was able to get away with her attention-seeking acts of evil for as long as she did.

**The Most Heinous Crimes**

On February 21 1991, little Liam Taylor was admitted to Ward 4 with an infection on his chest. Nurse Beverley reassured the seven-month-old's parents that he was in safe hands and even managed to convince them that they ought to go home and catch up on some sleep. When they got some rest and a change of clothes, they returned to the hospital to be met with Beverley telling them Liam had encountered a respiratory emergency, but he was recovering. The ever-concerned nurse volunteered to stay as an extra hand for the night shift so she could keep an eye on the youngster. The parents stayed at their little boy's side this time, too.

Liam endured another respiratory emergency late that night but yet again pulled through. At one point, Beverley was left alone with the poorly child. This was when his condition went from bad to much, much worse. The child went deathly white, and red blotches dotted across his pale face. Allitt requested the help of the emergency resuscitation team.

Beverley's colleagues all expressed their confusion as to why the alarm monitors didn't sound off when Liam stopped breathing. The boy had suffered cardiac arrest and, although the attending team did their best, he was left with permanent, severe brain damage and was being kept alive on life support. After speaking with medical experts, Liam's parents made the heartbreaking decision to take him off the life support machine. Heart failure was recorded as the cause of death, and Beverley was never questioned about Liam's sudden death, despite a number of things not adding up.

A fortnight after Liam Taylor's tragic death, Beverley struck yet again. Timothy Hardwick was an 11-year-old with cerebral palsy, admitted to hospital on March 5 1991, after an epileptic fit. The murderous nurse took him into her care and, after being left alone with the boy for a short while, requested the aid of the emergency resuscitation team. When they arrived, they found the boy blue without a pulse. They tried to revive him to no avail. Liam's subsequent autopsy failed to provide an accurate cause of death.

The third victim was Kayley Desmond, a one-year-old who was admitted to Ward 4 at the beginning of March 1991 after suffering from a chest infection. Her stay in the hospital seemed to help her condition improve, and recovery seemed to be speedy for the youngster. However, this all changed on her fifth day on the ward. Little Kayley suddenly went into cardiac arrest - in the same bed tragic Liam had died mere days before. Yet again the baby only fell ill when in the sole care of Beverley Allitt and the resuscitation team were called in. This time, however, they thankfully managed to revive the little girl. With a stroke of luck, she was sent to another hospital in Nottingham to be taken care of. Here, the physicians discovered a puncture hole under one of her armpits. They found an air bubble near the needle mark but there was no investigation into this.

Paul Crampton would be Nurse Allitt's next young victim with the five-month-old being placed in Ward 4 in March 1991 due to a bronchial infection. Just before he was due to be released, Beverley was yet again tending to a patient by herself and history would repeat itself with her summoning for help as little Paul suffered insulin shock, almost going into a coma on three different instances. The doctors managed to revive him each time but were baffled by the odd fluctuation in his insulin levels. He was then driven by ambulance to a different hospital in Nottingham, but the little boy was far from harm's way - Beverly Allitt decided to chaperone Paul and rode beside him. When they arrived at the new hospital, he was yet again found to have too much insulin. Despite Beverly's best attempts, baby Paul survived the attempts on his life from the woman soon to be dubbed the Angel of Death.

Still, Beverley Allitt wouldn't lay low after this - the very next day she struck again.

Five-year-old pneumonia sufferer Bradley Gibson would be her next vulnerable target. He went into sudden cardiac arrest but was luckily saved by the fast-moving resuscitation team. Blood tests would show his insulin levels being extremely high, which struck attending physicians as bizarre. Still, they'd stabilised the youngster - for now. A late-night visit from Nurse Allitt resulted in the child having another heart attack. Fortunately, he was sent to Nottingham, where he made a full recovery.

It's amazing to think that, despite the disturbing increase of incidents in the presence of one particular nurse - Allitt - no suspicions were voiced, and she was able to resume her spree of attacks on innocent children.

On March 22, 1991, toddler Yik Hung Chan suffered a sudden decline in health. He turned blue and was inconsolable, with no nurses able to explain the drastic change in his behaviour. He responded well when he was given oxygen but yet again when he was left with evil Allitt, he suffered another strange attack. The hospital made the decision to send him to Nottingham, where he recovered. They attributed his decline in health to a fractured skull.

Barely two-month-old twins Katie and Becky Phillips had been kept in hospital since their premature birth. Cautious doctors wanted to observe them to make sure they were sent home with a clean bill of health. However, a nasty case of stomach flu saw Becky enter Ward 4 on April Fools Day, 1991. Unfortunately, the nurse put in charge of their care was Beverley Allit. It only took two days for the nurse to yet again raise the alarm and summon the emergency team to help one of the babies. Little Becky's blood sugar was incredibly low, and she was cold to the touch. Still, nothing sinister was found, and the baby was cleared to go home with her mum. Even at a safe distance from evil nurse Allitt, Becky was still in danger. That same night, the child went into convulsions and was clearly in a lot of pain. She was rushed to the doctor who advised it was likely colic causing the cries. Her parents didn't leave her side the entire night, and the little girl sadly passed away during the early hours. Pathologists didn't manage to come to a clear reason for the premature death.

Katie, Becky's surviving sister, was immediately admitted to the hospital merely as a precaution, unaware that the cause of all of the death and anguish was waiting for them there. Unfortunately for little Kaire, Nurse Beverley was again tasked with the responsibility of taking care of her. After a short while alone with the baby, predictably Beverley summoned the resuscitation team to attend to Katie, who was no longer breathing.

Thankfully, the team's efforts to revive the tot were successful, although 48-hours later, the child endured a similar attack, which this time collapsed her little lungs. Yet another revival ensued, after which Katie was sent to Nottingham to recover, where the nurses made some sickening discoveries. Five of her tiny ribs were broken, and it was found that she suffered brain damage due to oxygen deprivation.

In a cruel and ironic twist, Katie's grateful mother, Sue Phillips, was overcome with gratitude and so beholden to Beverley for saving her little one's life that she took her aside and asked her to be Katie's godmother. The offer was accepted willingly. Despite Beverley having caused partial paralysis, irreparable sight and hearing damage and inflicting cerebral palsy on the baby, the sadistic nurse was more than happy to be given the title of godmother.

Another four victims followed in the same pattern as always. However, the high level of unexplained illnesses and attacks in otherwise healthy children coupled with Beverley Allitt's presence during each episode was formally raised as suspicious within the hospital. Her reign of terror over vulnerable children came to an end on April 22, 1991, when she caused the death of Claire Peck, who was little more than a year old. Claire was severely asthmatic and needed a breathing tube. After being left alone with the sadistic nurse for a short while, she suffered a heart attack. Cue Beverley calling on the resuscitation team yet again, who stabilised the child. Frustratingly, Claire was yet again left in the sole care of Beverly Allitt. The baby suffered another heart attack, one that she would not bounce back from. Revival attempts were futile.

The autopsy suggested that little Claire died from natural causes. However, hospital consultant Dr Nelson Porter suspected foul play and initiated an inquiry into the child's death. He was, quite rightly, disturbed by the extremely high number of heart attacks suffered by infants over the past two months on Ward 4. Subsequent tests revealed high levels of potassium in Claire's blood. Police were later called in to help with the investigation, resulting in the baby being exhumed. It was discovered the baby had traces of a local anaesthetic called Lignocaine in her system; this drug was never to be used to treat babies.

Superintendent Clifton was assigned to this upsetting investigation, immediately suspecting foul play. He ensured that the other suspicious deaths from the prior two months were looked into thoroughly and was in equal parts disgusted yet relieved to know the children all had incredibly high doses of insulin in their systems; the macabre discovery meant he could pursue the sick culprit. He had his suspicions as to who that could be. More sleuthing revealed that Beverley had reported the key to the insulin refrigerator as being missing. Subsequently, all insulin records were combed through, the parents of all victims were spoken to, and Ward 4 had cameras installed to check on all workers. The net, finally, was closing in.

The checks on the records revealed there were missing daily nursing logs, which tied in with the exact time period when Paul Crampton had been in Ward 4. These logs showed 25 suspicious episodes with a total of 13 victims identified, sadly four of whom had died. The common denominator? Beverley Allitt.

**The Arrest is Finally Made**

Towards the end of July 1991, the police were sure they had enough damning evidence to charge the wicked nurse Allitt with murder, but it took until November that year for her to be formally charged. She was unnervingly calm and restrained under heavy interrogation, and despite all of the evidence stacked against her, she denied any part in causing harm to the children of Ward 4. She insisted she'd done nothing but care for the victims, saying she'd done her best to save them.

A subsequent search of her home uncovered the missing segments from the nursing log. An extensive background check on Allitt showed a pattern of harmful and attention-seeking behaviour that suggested she had a personality disorder. She clearly exhibited symptoms of Munchausen's syndrome, which is a psychological disorder that sees the person feign illnesses or deliberately produce symptoms of illnesses in themselves. She also showed strong signs of having Munchausen syndrome by proxy, which sees the caregiver make up or deliberately causes illness or injury in a person under their care. It's been noted that it's unusual for someone to have both conditions, although Allitt seems to be one of the exceptions to this.

Her behaviour throughout adolescence was typical of someone with Munchausen's syndrome, and it seems like when these behaviours didn't evoke the desired reactions in others, she turned on the helpless young patients entrusted in her care. In order to satisfy her yearning for attention, she took to snuffing out the lives of those most vulnerable.

Numerous healthcare professionals visited Allitt while she was in prison, and she still wouldn't confess to her crimes. After a string of hearings, she was charged with four counts of murder, 11 of attempted murder, and a further 11 of causing grievous bodily harm. While waiting for her trial, she lost a noticeable amount of weight in a very short time, and it was revealed that she'd developed anorexia while behind bars, losing a total of five stone.

The Trial Begins

Delay after delay ensued due to Allitt's illness, made up or self inflicted. Eventually, realising that the trial was always going to be looming, she attended the trial at Nottingham Crown Court on February 15, 1993.

Prosecutors showed the jury the pile of evidence; how Allitt had been the only one present at each episode, how there were no episodes when she was no longer on the ward and how there was insulin and potassium found in all of her innocent victims. They pointed out how there were injection puncture marks present and accused the former nurse of cutting off some of the children's oxygen by maliciously tampering with their machines.

Her behaviour as a child was also brought up with prosecution bringing in Professor Roy Meadow to offer the jury an explanation of Munchausen syndrome and Munchausen by proxy, using it to describe how Allitt expressed symptoms of both. They also mentioned her post-arrest actions too, pointing to the high levels of illness she apparently endured, which caused delays to the trial. Professor Meadows said he thought that it was unlikely Beverley Allitt would be cured of these disorders, meaning she'd always be a danger to others.

The trial lasted almost two months, although Allitt herself only attended just over two weeks of it due to persistent illnesses. She was convicted on May 23, 1993, and handed 13 life sentences for the murder of four children and the attempted murder of five others. At the time, it was the most severe sentence ever given to a woman, but the judge noted that it was wholly in proportion to the suffering of her young victims, the unrelenting anguish it caused their families, and the way it tarnished the nursing profession for some time. The severity of the scandal saw the Grantham & Kesteven Hospital Maternity Unit close down completely.

Instead of going straight to jail, Beverley Allitt was sent to Rampton Secure Hospital in Nottingham to be incarcerated. It's a high-security unit that mainly houses those who've been detained under the Mental Health Act and offers much more freedom and luxury than prison. While at Rampton, it didn't take long for her to begin her attention-seeking behaviour yet again, going as far as ingesting ground glass and scolding her hands with boiling water. It was only here she subsequently admitted to carrying out three of the murders that she was charged for, alongside six of the violent attacks she carried out on her victims.

It's thought she'll never be eligible for release.

# Cynthia Coffman

The story of Cynthia Coffman reads like the script for the movie *Natural Born Killers*, where a couple embarks on a crime and killing spree. The protagonists are so in love with one another - and disregard human life so much - that the murders and horrific crimes they commit only seem to bring them closer together. It's hard to imagine what would drive a person to kill, aside from self-defence, especially when the victims are strangers to the murderer. For Cynthia Coffman and her boyfriend, it seems a mutual lust for blood brought them together and saw them set off on a murderous road trip, just like a plot from a straight to DVD b-movie.

Cynthia Coffman was born in 1962, brought up as a church-going, God-fearing Catholic. Her father was a successful businessman in St. Louis, and Cynthia had everything a young child would want materialistically. Although perhaps on the strict side, her upbringing wasn't unusual, and Cynthia was a happy child by all accounts. That all changed when she entered her teens.

Her religion meant that abortion wasn't ever an option for her, so she abided by her faith when she became pregnant at seventeen and entered a loveless marriage. Cynthia stood by the father of her child and the man she didn't love for five years before eventually fleeing the marital home in her early twenties. She took off with nothing but her car and the clothes she was wearing, driving west, eventually settling in Page, Arizona. To support herself, she took a job as a waitress in a diner and found herself a roof over her head a few weeks later when she met a local man with whom she moved in with. However, this wasn't a heartwarming, American love story; the pair would trash their apartment, have all-night parties and make enemies of their neighbours due to their loud antics. By autumn 1985, they were sent packing from the apartment.

Things carried on much the same for the pair, with parties, drinking, and causing a stir wherever they went. This lasted until May 8, 1986, when Cynthia and her boyfriend were caught running a stop sign in San Bernardino County, California. When searching the vehicle, police discovered a loaded handgun and a stash of methamphetamine in Cynthia's purse, but charges against her were eventually dropped. Her boyfriend wouldn't receive such leniency however - he ended up spending six weeks in county jail. Unbeknown to him, his stint behind bars led Cynthia to the man who would go on to change her life forever. He introduced her to his cellmate, James Gregory Marlow, who was there for stealing the car of his sixth wife. The 29-year-old man had been a criminal for most of his life, beginning with theft as a ten-year-old and escalating from there. He ended up being sent to Folsom Prison in 1980 for violent home invasions involving a knife.

James Marlow earned himself the moniker 'The Folsom Wolf' while showing off his tattoos that pledged alliance to the neo-Nazi Aryan Brotherhood. Still, this didn't faze Cynthia; for the pair of them, it was love at first sight as they caught eyes across the prison visitation room. James Marlow was the love of Cynhia's life; she just knew it. She blew off her boyfriend, and as soon as James was released, she met up with him and they hit the road to California together.

James had family living in the Southern Border, and he and Cynthia worked their way through every family member he had, taking what they could get from each one, sapping their resources dry before hopping onto the next well-meaning victim. Before moving on, the pair would be sure to take any valuables or anything they thought they could sell.

It wasn't too long before Marlow's relatives saw the pair coming a mile off, each turning them away when they turned up at their doorstep, often with shouts of profanity or perhaps sometimes a handful of pocket money just to get the two of them to get on their way. With every extortion avenue depleted, the couple resigned themselves to the fact they had nowhere to sleep but the woods. Far from a wayward lover's paradise, the woods were an uncomfortable, unhygienic place to call home. Cynthia struggled to rid herself of head lice while James bathed in kerosene to try to rid himself of berry bugs and their incessant biting.

On July 26, 1986, Cynthia and James were sick of living the way they were and turned to crime to dig them out of the hole they'd got themselves in. They burgled a home in Whitley County, Kentucky, taking a wad of cash, jewellery, as well as a shotgun. With their newfound windfall, mere days later the couple married in Tennessee. Cynthia commemorated the event by having a special tattoo inked on her buttocks. Etched across her posterior were the words: *I belong to the Folsom Wolf.* After marrying and basking in the subsequent after-party, they drifted towards the west again, looking to fund their free and easy life with yet another robbery spree; or perhaps, they spoke of carrying out even worse crimes to ensure no witnesses were left behind.

## A Series of Kidnappings and Murders

On the cool evening of October 11, 32-year-old Sandra Nearz left her house in Costa Mesa, California, and headed to the ATM to draw out some cash. She never returned from the quick trip out, and her car was discovered seemingly abandoned in a local car park. Almost a fortnight passed with no sign of Sandra until October 24 when horrified hikers in Riverside County stumbled upon her strangled, decomposing corpse.

Pamela Simmons, an Arizona woman in her mid-30s, was reported missing on October 28 in Bullhead City. Her car was later found near police HQ, a brazen place to leave evidence although it's not certain the person - or people - who snatched Pamela knew the area well enough to know this. Police concluded that she was abducted while taking money from the nearby ATM, but that was as far as their leads took them.

Less than two weeks later on November 7, Corinna Novis disappeared in similar circumstances in Redlands, California. The 20-year-old had been snatched from a bustling shopping mall in broad daylight. Despite the urban setting, there were no real leads or witnesses - yet again, police hit a dead end and were stumped.

Lynel Murray's boyfriend knew something was wrong when she didn't meet him for a date on November 12. The 19-year-old psychology student was supposed to meet him after she finished work, and it wasn't like her to be flaky or not show up as promised - something was most definitely up. He headed to her workplace and found her car parked outside the dry cleaning shop where she'd finished her shift but seemingly not headed anywhere. A day would pass before her sexually assaulted, naked, strangled body was found in a motel room on Huntington Beach. Police needed a break, just something to help them find the culprit. Fortunately, it wasn't much longer before the breadcrumbs of clues began dropping in front of them, leading them right to the killers.

Corinna Novis' chequebook was uncovered carelessly tossed in a Laguna Niguel dumpster, inside a takeout bag with papers crumpled up inside with some important evidence written on them: the full names of Cynthia Coffman and James Marlow. Around the same time, Marlow and Coffman were linked to a motel room in San Bernardino, where the manager reported discovering stationery with practice signatures of the name Lynel Murray, the same girl who'd vanished not too long ago. A statewide alert was sent out for the pair of fugitives.

By November 14 that year, police were called to attend a mountain lodge situated at Big Bear City, California, where the owner named and identified his latest guests as James Marlow and Cynthia Coffman. A posse of 100 men was assembled, but they found it empty once they stormed the lodge in question. They quickly dispersed to the nearby woods, fanning out in search of the murderous couple on the run. The search bore fruit quite quickly - at around 3:00 pm, the suspects were seen hiking on the mountain road. Armed police swarmed in, and the killer duo surrendered without a hint of a fight, both donning outfits they'd stolen from the dry cleaners where Lynel Murray had worked.

## The Extent of the Depravity is Revealed

Within hours of being apprehended, Cynthia caved and led officers to a vineyard not far from Fontana, California, where she showed them the sodomised, abused and strangled dead body of Corinna Novis laid in a crude, shallow grave.

On November 17, the pair were formally charged with Corinna's murder and were held for trial without bond. Not that any more proof of their guilt was needed, investigators also found fingerprints from both defendants inside their victim's car, and Cynthia used her real ID when she pawned the victim's typewriter for cash.

Two and a half years would pass by before the killers attended the trial, but during that time, they had a rough falling-out which caused each of them to blame the other for the crimes. Their relationship was confirmed dead when Cynthia's lawyer visited her in jail and asked if she needed anything from the outside. She told him there was something she needed and pointed to her derriere; "Find someone to help me lose this damn tattoo!" she demanded. Regardless of what the tattoo said, she was no longer the property of the so-called *Folsom Wolf*.

The duos murder trial started in San Bernardino County on July 18, 1989. The pair were convicted across the board, and both criminals were sentenced to death on August 30 that year. This made Cynthia Coffman the first woman to be sentenced to death in California since the state restored capital punishment in 1977. While she's still on death row as of 2021, it doesn't seem likely that California will be putting any new convicts to death any time soon.

# Myra Hindley

In the UK, Myra Hindley's name is still as reviled today as it was back in the 60s. Growing up, I saw her picture in the paper quite often, and her infamous mugshot with ice-white hair and a cold glare into the camera was frequently used on the news. Even as a seven-year-old, not quite understanding what the news reporter was talking about, I still knew the woman in the picture was to be feared. It was a stony face that looked like a cartoon villain, perhaps like a stony-faced Cruella, as she stared at me from the TV set. I could tell this woman had evil in her. Despite my young age, I wasn't wrong.

On the early mild morning of October 7, 1965, 17-year-old David Smith sat nervously in an inquiry room at Hyde Police Station alongside his young wife. The pair had turned up at the station that day with an almost unbelievable story. Superintendent Bob Talbot, who picked up the job of interviewing the couple, didn't yet know what he was about to stumble into; that he was going to become involved in a case so depraved and shocking that decades later, Britain still reels over it. The case would go on to be known as the Moors Murders.

When Superintendent Talbot entered the inquiry room to speak to the distressed teens, he found them nervously drinking tea, looking anxious yet ready to tell someone about the crimes that had clearly disturbed them so much. David Smith, comforted by his wife Maureen, went on to tell his shocking story.

The night before, David's sister-in-law, Myra Hindley, had dropped in to see him, Maureen and her mother. After a cup of tea and a catch-up, Myra was ready to set off home, but stalled; she said she was afraid to walk home by herself in the darkness, so David agreed to accompany her on the walk back to the home she shared with her partner, Ian Brady. When the pair arrived at 16 Wardle Brook Avenue, on the outskirts of Manchester, she asked David to come in as Ian had some bottles of wine for him to take back home. He entered the property and stood in the kitchen, scanning the labels on the wine that had been gifted to him, when he almost dropped the glass bottle he was holding; a blood-curdling scream came from the living room. The teen composed himself and entered the living area, shocked to see Ian with a life-size doll on the sofa. After close inspection, David realised the human-like doll wasn't a doll after all - it was a bloodied, dying man.

The beaten man fell to the floor, face down. Ian, axe in hand, stood over him. The victim was letting out slight groans as Brady lifted the sharp, bloody axe over his head and violently let it thud down on the incapacitated man. He lifted the weapon and did it again, this time screaming at the man, telling him he was a "dirty bastard." Myra, standing by watching, agreed with this. The man was in fact, the messiest victim they'd had so far, and let David know this. After some slight gurgling, the man stopped any kind of noise or movement.

Myra then took to the kitchen to make them all a hot cup of tea, joking with her partner about the terrified look on the young man's face when Ian had taken the axe to him. The pair laughed and joked as they told a nervous David about another

time when they were burying another victim on Saddleworth
Moor when a policeman turned up and questioned what they
were doing. Ian had previously told David that he'd murdered
before, but David brushed it off as a sick story he'd made up.
But he couldn't deny that what was happening right in front of
him was real. He was sick to his stomach and rightly feared for
his own safety.

He quickly decided to go along with the murderous pair and
act as cool as he could about the situation. He helped clean up
the bloody mess, gather the body, tie it up and put the corpse
in the spare bedroom. It took David until the early hours of the
morning to find the courage to escape, promising the twisted
pair that he'd return later that day to help properly dispose of
the dead man. Once he was back at home, the teen was violently sick before telling Maureen everything he'd seen and done
that night. Utterly panicked, the pair headed to a phone box to
call the police.

Superintendent Talbot went with Detective Sergeant Carr to
the Wardle Brook Avenue address where Myra and Ian had
supposedly axed a man to death. Over twenty extra police officers were called to the area in case of a nasty confrontation,
but surprisingly that didn't happen. Myra, rather unwillingly,
gave Talbot a key to the spare bedroom, which happened to
be the only locked room in the house. The superintendent was
shocked at the discovery - David had been telling the truth. The
brutalised body of a young man was laid on the floor wrapped
in a blanket. The murder weapon described by David was also
in the room.

The police swooped in on Ian Brady to arrest him immediately. At the police station, he told police a very different version of events than they'd already heard. He said that there was an argument between himself, David and the 17-year-old victim named Edward Evans. Subsequently, a fight ensued, which quickly escalated. David got the better of Edward, punching him to the ground and kicking him several times. Ian described a hatchet on the floor, which was used to hit the victim with. Ian stressed that he and David alone had tied the teenager up and moved him upstairs - Myra was in no way involved.

Myra was questioned too, but her version of events supported Brady's, detailing how she was frightened by the fighting and commotion. She wasn't arrested straight away, but four days later, police found a lengthy document written by her that went into explicit detail about how she and Brady were planning a murder. She was brought in again and questioned.

The investigation would likely have ended there if David hadn't divulged how Ian had told him about burying bodies on Saddleworth Moor. They were just scratching the surface of this killer couple's crimes.

## The Police Investigation Begins

Patricia Hodges, a twelve-year-old girl, told police how she often went with Myra and Ian to the moors to have a picnic, a story which was corroborated by the numerous photos discovered at the Brady home. From David's vague description of where the pair hid the bodies alongside the areas the little girl described going with Myra and Ian, police pinpointed likely areas where the evil couple could have buried their victims. The digging soon began.

Police suspected that the bodies of four missing children from the past few years might have been buried on the moors. They weren't wrong. October 10 rolled around, and the police discovered the body of Lesley Anne Downey. The 10-year-old had disappeared suddenly on Boxing Day, 1964. Less than two weeks after the first macabre discovery, the tiny body of John Kilbride was uncovered. The 12-year-old boy had disappeared without warning two years prior, in November 1963.

Britain in the 60s couldn't comprehend such a disturbing case. Nothing quite like it had ever happened, nothing that had ever been reported in the press anyway. This case was as unique as it was horrifying, with a woman being part of a killer duo slaying children and sexually abusing them. A female's involvement seemed to make the vile crimes even more evil and incomprehensible.

The big question on everyone's minds was, what made this young couple act in such a depraved and violent way? Ian Brady's childhood story was filled with abuse, and he was a troubled teenager, no stranger to the law. However, Myra had a "normal" childhood with nothing occurring that might trigger a future serial killer and child abuser. What happened to this woman to cause her to gain pleasure from the sexual abuse and slaughter of young children?

Born on July 23, 1942, in an industrial area of Manchester to Bob and Nellie Hindley, Myra was raised predominantly by her mother as her father was often away serving in the parachute regiment. They lived with Myra's grandmother, Ellen Maybury, who took care of Myra while Nellie was at her machinist job. When Bob returned from his army duties, they bought their own property around the corner from Nellie's mother. Bob struggled with civilian life and would spend most of his time in the local pub when he wasn't labouring. Maureen, the couple's second child, was born in the late summer of 1946, but seeing as Bob and Nellie both worked full time, they struggled with two young children. Myra was sent back to live with her grandmother.

The move to her gran's appeared to have solved a number of Myra's family's issues - Granny Ellen was no longer by herself, Bob and Hettie were relieved that they had one less mouth to feed, and young Myra revelled in the attention she got living with her grandmother. However, it also meant that Myra never got to have a fully fleshed-out relationship with her dad. Couple this with the fact that the man wasn't particularly affectionate with his children, and it could be that Myra felt there was a gap where a father's love ought to be.

Myra started primary school at five and was seen as a mature little girl who was eager to learn by her teachers, despite her grandmother's tendency to keep her at home at a whim. Her high number of absences caused her to fail in getting the grades needed to attend the nearby grammar school, so she had no choice but to attend the local secondary school. Her scatty attendance would continue here, but she was always in the top classes for most subjects anyway. Her teachers noted that Myra exhibited a talent for creative writing and enjoyed writing poetry. She was athletic, took part in sports and was a keen swimmer. Her appearance wasn't considered to be too feminine by her peers, and her broad hips and hooked nose attracted cruel name-calling.

When she was 15, Myra became closer friends with Michael Higgins, a 13-year-old who was incredibly shy, timid and somewhat fragile. She looked out for her friend and protected him from cruel taunts and bullying in an older sibling type of way. Myra knew, no matter what, that they would be friends forever. One day, she was supposed to meet him to go swimming in the local reservoir but decided to go meet some other friends instead. Michael decided to go swimming alone anyway. When he drowned that day, the pain she felt was made worse by the guilt she felt for not going swimming with him; if she had, she was a strong enough swimmer that she could have saved him from the trouble he got himself into. The guilt ate young Myra up.

The following weeks saw Myra flit between hysterical and being quietly depressed. She sobbed, she screamed, she made frequent trips to church to light candles for Michael, she collected a fund for his wreath, she dressed solely in black. Her family saw her behaviour as an overreaction. After this trauma, her schoolwork deteriorated, and she dropped out, leaving education without qualifications.

She entered the working world as a clerk at Lawrence Scott and Electrometers in a junior position. Despite dealing with all-encompassing grief, she started to act like other people her age. She would go to dances, listen to Elvis, flirt with the boys her age and partook in smoking behind the bus stops and bike sheds. As with most teens, her appearance became of utmost importance, and she decided her look would be bleach blonde hair and heavy eye makeup. Perhaps intentionally, this served to make Myra look much older than the relatively naive teen she was.

When she turned seventeen, she got engaged to a local teen called Ronnie Sinclair, a tea-blender at the corner shop. Myra' contentment - or what seemed like it, anyway - with her rather bland life did not last long at all. Just thinking about her pending nuptials caused Myra to seriously doubt the lifestyle ahead of her should she get married to Ronnie. After exchanging vows, you bought a small property, then you had children, struggled to make ends meet, had to deal with a drunken, philandering husband, then you both died. This filled a young Myra with dread. She called off the wedding.

She needed excitement, and although she didn't quite know what that looked like, she searched for it anyway. She got application forms for the army and the navy, filling them out but going no further with them. She had dreams of going to America, working as a nanny to initially get her over there, but this was yet another idea that never came to fruition. London called her name too, but she couldn't get a job there. Before she knew it, a couple of years had passed and she was treading water with no excitement in sight. This drought would last until January 1961, when she clapped eyes on Ian Brady, who began working at the same place as Myra.

Unbeknown to an instantly besotted Myra, this first encounter was the start of a fatal attraction. While other people would think of Brady as rather sullen and quite quick-tempered, Myra viewed this as him being the strong, silent type who was mysterious and aloof. His withdrawn nature saw Myra believe Ian was intelligent and someone special as he was a stark contrast to any of the guys she'd dated. Ian Brady made Ronnie Sinclair look dull, unambitious and childish. Myra's diary exposed her deep longing for Brady, which would remain a secret for quite some time - her object of affection remained disinterested in the lovestruck woman for a whole year.

At the work Christmas party, Ian had downed a few drinks, giving him the courage to ask Myra on a date. Relaxed by a few drinks, they arranged their date. The first one on one time they had was to see The Nuremberg Trials, beginning Myra's journey into his mysterious world. It wasn't long before Ian played his date recordings of Hitler's marching songs and strongly encouraged her to read Mein Kampf. Keen to impress the man she'd longed for for so long, she complied. She had wanted excitement, and now it had arrived. Her naivety and yearning for something out of the ordinary saw Myra unable to distinguish between normal behaviours and dangerous ones. Ian Brady soon became Myra's lover, and she was undeniably besotted.

All she wanted to do was please her new boyfriend. She began adopting Germanic style in her dress, donning long boots with mini skirts. She'd indulge him in his fetishes, allowing him to take nude, intimate photographs of her, including shots of the two having sex. As time went on, Ian's thoughts became increasingly paranoid, but this didn't bother Myra; in fact, she found herself falling into his ideologies. He told her that God didn't exist, so she stopped attending church. Unbelievably, when he announced that murder and rape weren't wrong, that they were supreme pleasures, she accepted this as truth. Her once headstrong personality soon intertwined with Ian's warped way of thinking.

These changes didn't go unnoticed by Myra's friends, family and coworkers. She became surly, unapologetically aggressive, and her "kinky" dress sense was hard to miss, particularly among her conservative peers. Maureen, Myra's sister would later testify in court that after she began dating Ian Brady, she became secretive, no longer spending time with friends or going to dances. The one-time babysitter also now said she hated children and people.

In 1963, Myra's blind acceptance of her boyfriend was to be put to the test. He was going to rob a bank and he wanted her to be the getaway driver. Straight away, Myra started taking driving lessons and bought some guns after joining the rifle club. The robbery never materialised, but Myra had proved to be willing to carry out whatever Ian wanted her to do, and with this in mind, the dangerous man was ready to escalate his depravity.

On the humid night of July 12, 1963, the couple snared their first victim, teenager Pauline Reade.

The sixteen-year-old was on her way to a dance before she suddenly vanished. Initially, she was going to attend with three friends, Pat, Linda and Barbara, but she had to make her own way to the venue alone when their parents stopped them from going after finding out alcohol was freely available there. Sociable Pauline didn't want to miss out on an event, so after dressing up in her favourite pink dress, she headed out the door to make the walk alone. Unbeknown to Pauline, two of her friends who were also on the way to the dance followed her partway, covertly watching her while seeing if she would actually have the nerve to attend a party on her own. After a while, the duo stopped trailing their friend and took a shortcut to the dance, hoping to get there before Pauline and tell her that they'd been trailing her. The two friends waited and waited, but Pauline never turned up at the dance.

Come midnight, Joan and Amos Reade set out to look for their daughter. She would never stay out this late. The next morning, when there was still no sign of Pauline, they called the police. A police search turned up nothing. Pauline, it seemed, had vanished into thin air.

Another child disappeared on November 11, 1963. John Kilbride and John Ryan had headed to the cinema to spend the afternoon there. After watching their film, they visited the local market to see if they could hustle a little money by offering to help the stall owners to pack up their goods. After a successful day for a pair of twelve-year-olds, John Ryan left to go home as his buddy John Kilbride waited for a bus beside a salvage bin. No one saw the young boy alive again, except for his evil captors.

With John's dinner left untouched on the table, his parents worried that their usually punctual son was in trouble. Sheila and Patrick Kilbride wasted no time in calling the police, resulting in another major search being conducted, seeing thousands of concerned volunteers join forces with the police to comb the local area for clues as to what happened to John. Frustratingly for all involved, not to mention the anguish the Kilbride's felt, no clues were found. All anyone knew was that John had disappeared.

Another child went missing six months after this. June 16, 1964, started out as a normal Tuesday for Keith Bennett, where the twelve-year-old would usually go to his grandmother's and sleep over. His grandmother's place was only a mile away from his own home, so he often walked himself there, as he did on this particular Tuesday. As usual, his mother watched him as he crossed the roads, ensuring he looked left and right. When she was confident he was safe, she headed in the opposite direction to go to bingo.

Keith didn't get to his grandmother's house. Winnie, although disappointed, didn't think much of this; she decided that his mother had changed her plans and didn't need to send young Keith to stay with grandma.

The following morning, Winnie went to visit her daughter's home. Both were expecting the other to have Keith. With the realisation that something potentially horrific had happened to the young boy, the police were called. Again, a search took place with the help of the local community, but people were now talking; yet another child had vanished without a trace.

Yet another six months rolled by before a fourth child, Lesley Ann Downey, suddenly disappeared. It was Boxing Day afternoon, 1964, when ten-year-old Lesley had tagged along with her two brothers and their friends to attend the local fair, a mere ten minute walk away from their home. It only took a few games of pick a duck and bean bag tossing for their collective pocket money to be spent up, and they were quickly bored. With little else to do, everyone headed home - except Lesley. She was last seen late that afternoon, standing by herself and observing the rides.

When Lesley didn't come home for dinner, her panicked mother Ann, along with stepdad Alan, set out searching for her. After spending hours scouring the local area, they called the police. As before, the countryside and surrounding areas were searched, with thousands of individuals being questioned in order to gain some clue or lead. Posters with Lesley Ann's face were printed and stuck up all over in the hopes that someone knew where she was or her captor somehow saw them and set the little girl free.

Another ten months would roll by before the horrifying truth of the situation was uncovered. The worst-case scenario was about to be realised.

## The Evidence Was Undeniably Damning

Lesley Ann's naked body was discovered lying in a makeshif
grave; her clothes strewed carelessly at her feet. Police had
nothing to guide them but hearsay and flaky circumstantial ev
idence that led them to Ian Brady and Myra Hindley as po
tential suspects in Lesley's murder. This wasn't enough; they
needed more before pursuing the pair. A subsequent thorough
search of their home on Wardle Brook Avenue on October 1
saw them find a trove of damning evidence.

A left-luggage ticket, tucked inside the pages of a prayer book
of all things, directed Manchester police to a locker at Central
station. Inside the locker were two suitcases filled with abhor
rent items, including sadistic pornography and paraphernalia
Strewn through these items were nine explicit photograph
of Lesley Ann Downey, depicting her as naked, tied up and
gagged in a number of pornographic poses in Myra Hindley'
bedroom. A disturbing tape recording was also among the se
lection of horrifying finds. The frightened and trembling voic
of a young girl could be heard as she was screaming, hysterical
crying, and pleading for her life. A male and female were also
heard, threatening the little girl with violence. This enabled po
lice to identify the adult voices as Ian Brady and Myra Hind
ley, but in a cruel twist for the girl's mother, they required
Ann Downey's help in identifying the screaming child's voice
She had to listen in sheer horror and anguish as her daughte
begged for her life in her final moments.

Despite the damning evidence piling high against the pair, Ian and Myra still denied murdering Lesley Ann. They attempted to implicate David Smith yet again, claiming that David had invited the girl to the house for Ian to take pictures of her. The recording police had heard was merely of their voices subduing the young girl so they could take their photos. Myra insisted that she was only harsh with the youngster because she was afraid the neighbours would hear her commotion. According to the pair, Lesley Ann had left their property alive and well with David Smith. They suggested that he must have murdered her when he was alone with her.

The evidence linking the couple to the murder of John Kilbride was not as damning but was thankfully still sufficient enough order to charge them with killing him. They found John Kilbride's name written in a notebook that was found in the pair's belongings, with the child's name written in Ian Brady's handwriting. There was also a photo of Myra on John's makeshift grave on the moors. It was also uncovered that Myra had hired a car the day John vanished, and when she brought it back to the showroom, it was notably muddy.

Still, police were unable to find the bodies of the other missing children and nor could they find any conclusive evidence to link the couple to their disappearance. They had to make do with the evidence they currently had, which enabled them to proceed with the murders of Edward Evans, Lesley Ann Downey, and John Kilbride.

On April 27, 1966, the callous couple were brought to trial, where they each pleaded not guilty to all charges brought against them. Even throughout the trial, they still placed the blame on David Smith for the killings, a cowardly act that only aided further public hatred towards them. At no point through the trial did either of them show a single shred of remorse for their horrific crimes or any emotion or guilt for the things they put families of their victims through. They exposed themselves for what they were: cold and heartless.

While Ian Brady was found guilty of killing Lesley Ann Downey, John Kilbride, and Edward Evans, Myra Hindley was found guilty of killing only Lesley Ann Downey and Edward Evans. For John Kilbride, she was guilty of harbouring her partner in the knowledge that he had killed the young boy.

Ian Brady's hold over Myra didn't wane, at least not for the first few years of imprisonment. They wrote to one another constantly and requested permission to marry. A rift slowly developed over the years, slowly but gradually, perhaps in part due to their differing reactions to their imprisonment. While Myra asserted her innocence and didn't settle into incarceration well, Ian accepted what he was handed and also accepted what everyone else was already certain of: his guilt. Hindley didn't relent on her insistence that her partner and David Smith were the real child killers and even tried to appeal. By 1970, she stopped contacting Ian Brady, knowing she'd never see him or be with him again. More than a decade after being imprisoned, Myra started a campaign for her freedom. Over the next few years, she wrote a comprehensive 20,000-word essay where she portrayed herself as the manipulated, abused and innocent victim of Ian Brady's overpowering personality.

The document was submitted to the Home Office, but parole board officials determined that it would be an additional three years before her application for parole could be considered.

## Myra Becomes More Forthcoming - But Only For Her Own Selfish Reasons

Her application for parole was again delayed another three years in 1982 by Home Secretary William Whitelaw. Her application was finally heard in 1985, two decades after her incarceration began; it was promptly rejected. Myra slowly realised her incessant claims of non-involvement in the child murders was implausible, to say the least. Before the end of 1986, Keith Bennett's mother wrote a letter to his killers, begging Myra to tell her what had happened to her son, perhaps providing the convict with a newfound inspiration for her early release tactics.

In early 1987, Myra made front-page news in the UK with the public release of her full confession to her involvement in all five murders, although she still insisted that she hadn't actually murdered any of the children - she was just the abused accomplice. Ian Brady's confession came soon after, devoid of any remorse.

The duo's confessions confirmed police belief that the bodies of Pauline Reade and Keith Bennett had been buried on the moors. Neither killer was able to lead police to the exact locations, although Pauline's remains were eventually located on July 1, 1987, sadly identifiable by the pink party dress she wore on the day she disappeared.

The couple's accounts of what happened leading up to Pauline's murder correlate, although not so much for their descriptions of Myra's role in it. Myra said she'd tricked the young girl into going to Saddleworth Moor with her by offering her a reward of some records should she help her find a glove she lost there. Once Myra and the young victim were on the moors, Ian Brady drove up on his motorbike and joined a helpful and innocent Pauline to look for the "missing glove" while Myra returned to the car and sat in the passenger seat. While alone with Pauline, Ian Brady had raped her and slit her throat before returning to Myra and asking her to help bury the child's body. Ian Brady disputed this account, insisting that his ex was much more active in not only the killing but the abuse and rape of the young girl too.

Keith Bennett's body was never uncovered, although Myra's confession offered up some sort of possible indication of how he died. She says she lured him into the car after asking the young boy for some help loading boxes. Once they arrived at Saddleworth Moor, Ian Brady led Keith to a small gully with a stream flowing through. Here, he raped the boy before strangling him to death, burying his body somewhere nearby the running water.

When describing the murder of Lesley Ann Downey, yet again Myra distances herself from the scene at the time of the killing, claiming to have retreated to the bathroom when the young girl was raped and strangled by Ian Brady. However, Brady's recollection is much different; he insists that it was Myra who performed the fatal strangulation with her bare hands. It's this version of events that most closely matches the audiotape recording of the murder, where the killer's voices are clearly heard.

Myra's solicitor expressed his confidence that her chances of a successful parole hearing were greater should she display remorse for her crimes, and he believed that she might succeed in being released in another ten years. With this at the forefront of her mind, and despite her earlier declaration that she would stop her plight for freedom, again, she applied for parole in 1986. This time, Home Secretary Michael Howard stressed that Hindley would never be released.

Myra Hindley passed away in 2002 due to respiratory failure, aged sixty. Ian Brady in 2017 of natural causes. He was seventy-nine.

***

Thank you for reading *Female Killers*.

As you can likely tell, I have a real interest in true crime and I soak up any news story, podcast, book or documentary that covers the tale of a horrific aspect of humanity.

Still, I was apprehensive about writing a book of my own and putting it out there, but I'm glad I did. Despite the macabre subject, I enjoyed sitting down each morning to work on this book (alongside other books I have planned). In writing this, I'm hoping to develop my own voice in the true crime commu-

nity and create quite a few books on true crime cases that have
really affected me over the years. I read true crime books rapid
ly and would like to contribute my take on these real-life storie
to enthusiasts like me. I'm a big believer in never forgetting the
shocking and disturbing parts of the past in the hope that we
can learn from them and remember the victims of such tragi
events. I hope this and my forthcoming books will serve to do
that.

I'd like to thank anyone who's listened to me chat abou
women killers over the past few months, and I appreciate you
taking the time to humour me in my dark and often morbid
questions, anecdotes and theories. I'd also like to thank my fel
low true crime writers who've helped me decide on what topic
to cover and what I need to do to keep sane while diving head
first into a new true crime writing venture.

Most of all, though, I'd like to thank you for making it this far
I hope that means you liked the book and I hope you've learned
about some new cases that have made you wonder what goe
through a killer's head as they snuff out the life of another hu
man being. For me, I found no sympathy, no real reason or ex
planation as to why most of these women chose to kill, with
the exception of Aileen Wuornos, for whom I did have a de
gree of sympathy for. I do not condone her horrific actions, bu
the abuse and mistreatment she endured go some way to ex
plain her shift from a beaten-down young girl to a murderou
woman.

The Karla Homolka case stuck with me for years, and when researching the case further, I unearthed some old tapes where she was showing police around her home. Instead of being cut up about the horrific things she'd done, she was more concerned about the police damaging her belongings. Her baby-like voice contradicts the pain and torture she inflicted on other women and it's frightening to know that there are people like this in the world - probably many more than we would like to acknowledge.

The most frustrating case was perhaps Beverley Allitt. The fact that she got away with murdering child after child, and left more than enough clues for even the most unassuming person to pick up on, is beyond me. There's no doubt whatsoever that if she wasn't caught she would have continued to slay young children, all for her own desire for attention.

There were more cases I'd liked to have covered in this book, but in keeping with the kind of books I want to write (relatively short, to the point, with all the important aspects of the cases covered), I had to stop when reaching around 35,000 words. I love the true crime genre, but for me, there are too many long-winded books that go over the criminal's grandparents and talk at length about their relationship with their mother. These thick books, despite having an abundance of fascinating information, are often left on my shelf a third of the way through, and I check the internet or seek out a shorter, more punchy book.

For book two, I'm currently delving into researching the Manson girls and Carol Bundy. Two wildly differing cases with two horrific tales behind the crimes. I'm looking forward to getting started!

I would be incredibly grateful if you left a review or a rating. It helps get my book out there and in front of new readers, which in turn helps me sit down and research and write more books. If you have anything at all to say about the book, a review is the best place to say it! I will certainly read and take note of every review I get.

For now, I'm excited to begin a book I've been researching for some time. It's called 'Copycat Killers' and it's about (you probably guessed it) copycat murderers. I've had to split the book into two so it's not too long; part one for murderers who took inspiration from the media and movies and part two for killers who copied other murderers. I hope to see you there!

Until then, take care.

Eliza

Manchester, England, February 2021

***

## About the Publisher

Dimension Books is a UK based non-fiction publisher specialising in true cime and intriguing real-life events.
Find us at Dimensionbooks.com and on social media.

# Acclaim for *Temptation*

"In Curtis Bracy's *Temptation: Your Destiny Signal*", he defines temptation as "a backstabbing self-esteem booster." He admits the negative aspects of temptation and then depicts how the struggles of temptation can propel you to the next level if dealt with wisely. Using the experiences of Joseph and Samson he gives the reader methodologies to overcome their personal inner battles. Giving practical advice he shows us the importance of using God's Word. The psychological turmoil, that occurs during periods of temptation can be overcome to boost us to the next level in Christ. Written in the language of lay people Bracy encourages us actively seek to overcome temptation, through God's unmerited favor."

-Deacon Alexander C. Stewart, BSMT, MTS

"This book does not only highlight God's saving power in helping us overcome the temptations that we all face daily. This book also delves into the reasons behind our desires and the things that entice us. When you read this book, you will gain a greater understanding of the spiritual implications of our decisions, how trauma sometimes influences our choices, and the reality of the struggles that we face as human beings who are seeking God's help to live for Him. I pray that as you flip through the pages you see yourself in every biblical account and in every encouraging word that is provided by Elder Curtis Bracy."

-Karen Sinfleur, Licensed Associate Counselor

"It is seldom that I read bodies of work that reflect the matters of our hearts that lead to repentance and redemption. While some write books to peak the human mind, Elder Bracy has written this book, as well as his others, to prick the heart, empower the mind, and convict our souls. Just as Jesus Christ taught in parables it is remarkable how God has graced Elder Bracy with the ability to convey simple concepts that lead to spiritual revelation. *Temptation* has been an extreme blessing to me. In most cases, we view temptation as an inward battle where we travail against the temptation that we must overcome. However, Elder Bracy goes even deeper, diving into the truth that temptation can be the luring potion that others ingest that will lead to insanity. People will attack you for no reason. They will talk about you all without cause. Why? Because they are tempted. It brings to mind James 1:13-15, which says, "Let no man say when he is tempted, I am tempted of God: for God cannot be tempted with evil, neither tempteth he any man: But every man is tempted, when he is drawn away of his own lust, and enticed. Then when lust hath conceived, it bringeth forth sin: and sin, when it is finished, bringeth forth death." Death is the price for being consumed by temptation. Not just a feeling. Not just a moment, but the spirit of temptation that will wreck your life. In all, Elder Bracy's book will definitely confirm to many, that God will send His servants to speak to generations in a language that they can understand. The amount of revelation that I've experienced has been monumental and I am thankful for his gift."

-Keiara B. Gladney, MPA, Licensed Evangelist,<br>
Founder of Charitea Movement